Mastering Personal Magnetism

Also by Dr. Dele Ola

Be a Change Agent: Leadership in a Time of Exponential Change

Pursuit of Personal Leadership: Practical Principles of Personal Achievement

Rip Off Your Blindfold: See How Successful People See

Mastering Personal Magnetism

HOW TO BECOME A LEADER PEOPLE WANT TO FOLLOW

Dr. Dele Ola

The Prowezz Company

Copyright © 2025 by Dr. Dele Ola

All rights reserved. No part of this publication may be reproduced or transmitted in any form or by any means—electronic or mechanical, including photocopying, recording or any information storage and retrieval system—without permission in writing from the publisher.

Published by The Prowezz Company, Inc., Ottawa, ON, Canada

Edited by Bobbi Beatty of Silver Scroll Services, Calgary, AB, Canada

Mastering Personal Magnetism / Dr. Dele Ola First Edition 2025

ISBN
978-1-7779645-8-0 (paperback)
978-1-7779645-9-7 (e-book)

1. *Self-Help / Communication & Social Skills*
2. *Self-Help / Personal Growth / Success*
3. *Business & Economics / Leadership*
4. *Self-Help / Motivational & Inspirational*

This book may be purchased in bulk at quantity discounts for corporate, educational, reselling, gifting, or promotional purposes through the author. Kindly visit www.deleola.com or call 1 (204) 421-4018 for more information.

DEDICATION

This book is especially dedicated

To those who would pursue the mastery of personal magnetism;

To my wife, Ruth; my daughter, Inioluwa; and my son, Iseoluwa—my support system;

And to Remi Adedapo, Tolu Sajobi, and Ope Onifade for offering their perspectives on the manuscript.

Contents

Introduction	1
1. Radiate a Captivating Presence	5
2. Recalibrate Your Mindset and Attitude	23
3. Exude Self-Belief and Confidence	43
4. Use the Power of Presence to Build Meaningful Connections	61
5. Embrace Success in All Facets of Life	79
6. Let Your Creativity and Innovation Speak	97
7. Be an Overcomer	113
8. Become an Efficient Self-Manager	135
9. Be Patient But Persist	155
10. Find Fulfillment and Happiness	171
Conclusion	185
About the Author	187
Notes	189

INTRODUCTION

Have you ever wondered how one particular person can captivate so many, as if they possess an enchanting magnetism that draws people in? I have met several delightful individuals. They command respect, ooze affection, and radiate affability. Those people may be described as charming, pleasant, or lovely.

People who naturally attract others don't always match the traditional definition of physical beauty. Nonetheless, some intangible quality makes them inherently lovable, collaborative, or friendly, and that makes them charming. This suggests that our desirability is influenced more by what we cultivate within ourselves than by our external appearance. An individual can possess physical beauty but still be challenging to connect with, while another may not have conventional attractiveness yet still be lovable and easy to be with or work with.

The personality you exude determines whether people will cling to you or resist you. No matter how physically handsome or beautiful you are, it takes an appealing personality to become a person people can love. No one becomes delectable just because they don fancy clothing and apply costly accessories. Real beauty comes first from the inside, and it radiates outward. Though someone may initially come across as likable due to their appealing physical appearance, it doesn't take long for that illusion to wear off.

Everyone can shape their personality. The way others perceive us is, in many cases, a direct result of how we have crafted that image. When I hear people complain that others just don't like them, I wonder if that is just an alibi for a lack of personal effort to become someone others enjoy being with. How can everyone at your place of work or in your community dislike you? It is improbable that everyone around dislikes you unless you are a victim of a conspiracy or misinformed collective resentment. Many of us need to consider how we allow others to view us. While we cannot dictate others' perceptions of us, we do have control over our presentation and the qualities we showcase.

Do you know anyone who is not friendly yet has a large circle of friends? Probably not. Friendly individuals tend to attract other friendly people. Similar attitudes draw people together. Affectionate people are surrounded by affectionate people. To cultivate friendships, we need to adopt friendly outward behaviors. Adopting intimidating demeanors, speaking insensitively, and being an authoritarian will not attract well-meaning individuals to you. If we want to attract good people, we must break our walls and step down from our mountaintops. Our words and actions must show others that we care about them. Do you treat your colleagues, family, and others around you well? When people look for someone to be with, to follow, would they choose you?

In today's fast-paced world, the ability to connect with others on a deeper level has never been more crucial. Personal magnetism is not just about being liked; it's about creating meaningful relationships that can lead to personal and professional success. A desirable and inviting personality can open doors to many opportunities. As individuals get closer to you and observe your admirable lifestyle and esteemed character, it naturally becomes easier for them to trust and connect with you.

Do you want to become a person or a leader who attracts and inspires others? Do you want to cultivate a personal appeal that makes you stand out from the crowd? Do you want to elevate yourself and achieve your goals with grace and poise? If you've read this far, you must, so you have picked the right book.

The journey to mastering personal magnetism is a deeply personal one, requiring introspection and a willingness to grow beyond one's comfort zone. Throughout this book, you will find practical tips and real-life examples to help you apply the necessary principles so you can master personal magnetism in your daily life. Whether you are looking to enhance your leadership skills, improve your social interactions, or simply become a more engaging individual, the lessons in this book will guide you every step of the way.

It is important to note that mastering personal magnetism is not a destination but a continuous journey. As you progress through the chapters, you will discover that the qualities that make you magnetic are also those that contribute to a fulfilling and balanced life. An appealing personality combines charm and kindness with achievement, confidence, resilience, creativity, self-management, satisfaction, and a positive attitude. As you progress on your journey, embrace the lessons, be patient with yourself, and enjoy your transformation. After reading this book, you will not only understand what it takes to be irresistibly captivating but also how to maintain and nurture these qualities throughout your life.

Take a moment to relax and clear your mind, then get your marker ready and immerse yourself in this rich compilation of knowledge and wisdom. I wish you enjoyment with each page you turn.

CHAPTER 1

RADIATE A CAPTIVATING PRESENCE

No matter who you are, no matter what you did, no matter where you've come from, you can always change, become a better version of yourself.

~ Madonna Ciccone ~

I had an interesting conversation with my close friend, Tolu, one day. We reminisced about our days in management consulting, roughly eighteen years earlier. During our talk, a former colleague's name came up. This individual joined our firm with considerable experience from another sector and was about a decade older than us. There was something fascinating about our new colleague. He commanded attention. He stood out because of his ability to draw people's focus. This person possessed a magnetic charm that garnered the admiration of every person in the company, from entry-level employees to the managing director. Tolu and I concurred that this colleague didn't outshine others in technical aptitude or business acumen. Nevertheless, his demeanor held an indescribable quality that made him a desirable team member. Both clients and staff held him in high regard, and his interactions with clients were so fluid it appeared as though he was part of their organization.

Reflecting on this, I couldn't help but ponder the extent to which his engaging personality played a role in our firm's collective achievements. How transformative would it be if most, or even all of us, could harness such captivating influence? What if we could all cultivate a personality that effortlessly drew people in? Through many years of working with others and developing myself, I've learned to project a compelling presence. Now I believe it's important to pass on the wisdom I've gained.

In this chapter, I share my insights, stories, and tips on developing a captivating presence that draws people to you and makes them desire your presence and contributions. You will learn the qualities and skills that make you a gracious, thoughtful, and effective person and leader. You will discover how to work on yourself, surround yourself with the best people, face challenges, lead with integrity and sportsmanship, and be a thought leader who is mindful of others. You will also find practical actions to help you apply these lessons and grow as a leader and a person.

Whether you are a seasoned leader or an aspiring one, this chapter will help you enhance your leadership style and impact and increase your personal magnetism.

Let's begin the journey of personal growth and leadership excellence with one of the most fundamental aspects of our relationship: being gracious when dealing with others.

Cultivate Graciousness and Courtesy

I find one thing fascinating. From an early age, we are taught to avoid engaging with strangers because of potential danger. It's commonplace for parents to caution their children, "Don't talk to strangers." Therefore, as we grow up, we learn to keep to ourselves. As a result, everywhere we go, even in public spaces like transit, it's often the same: people refrain from talking to strangers for fear of encountering someone with ill intentions. Not knowing someone categorizes them as a stranger; thus, we often choose not to engage. While it's true that there are malicious individuals out there, there are also many benevolent ones.

As we get to know others, our perceptions begin to shift. A stranger can eventually become a friend. Everyone in your life was once a stranger, even family members. Relationships are formed and built over time through interaction and shared experiences. Our opinions of the people we work with or surround ourselves with are also formed over time.

Our perceptions of others, coupled with our willingness to get to know them, is the foundation of fostering positive relationships and being cherished in return. People tend to shy away from those who do not show an interest in them. Yet the renowned theologian, John Wesley, notably stated, "We should be rigorous in judging ourselves and gracious in judging others." A distinctive quality in likable individuals and effective leaders is their graciousness. Gracious people are kind and agreeable, extending the benefit of the doubt during first encounters and forgiving mistakes simply due to human imperfection.

In my day-to-day life, I strive to maintain a positive outlook with people. I've found that the more positive I am toward others, the more positively I'm perceived by them. I aim to stay positive even if the sentiment isn't always reciprocated. When I'm faced with issues that could affect my relationships, I remind myself of the bigger picture and what's truly important. I remind myself I must avoid getting lost in trivial issues and that I must move forward with forgiveness and understanding.

Being accepting and gracious is an art applicable across various aspects of life. Gracious individuals can provide sincere critiques while remaining kind. Whether it's correcting their children, managing their staff, or interacting with people they encounter, they do so with grace. Reflect on your life path and your wish to maintain good relationships with those around you and ask yourself how gracious you truly are. Would those connected to you describe you as someone who embodies graciousness?

One significant benefit of acting graciously is fostering trust and unity. ***When people feel confident in your gracious nature, they will be more open to you.*** They will know your grace will extend to them when they make mistakes. The journey to becoming gracious and imparting courtesy contributes enormously to cultivating personal appeal and influence.

Although being gracious to everyone who crosses your path is an important starting point on the journey to mastering the art of personal magnetism, becoming a better version of yourself is equally crucial. Let us look at this briefly.

Elevate Yourself

If humans were computer software, I'd ask, "Which version are you?" So ask yourself, are you still the original version, or have you progressed to an updated version? Consider the last time you purposefully developed a new aspect of your social abilities. How would you describe your path of personal evolution? In the previous section, I addressed graciousness. Let's contemplate other qualities now, such as communication, patience, emotional regulation, alertness, generosity, and similar traits. These personal qualities are key to mastering an attractive persona. Without committing to continual self-improvement and seizing every chance to upgrade ourselves, our potential to attract and captivate others will be limited.

Our capability to draw people in, initiate change, accomplish significant deeds, and sway others so we can achieve positive outcomes hinges not only on our vision and internal drive but also on our capacity. Typically, without external assistance, we realize only what is within our perceived personal capacity. Your perceived capacity limits what you can hold, create, or attain. For instance, the extent of physical energy you can exert, or the labor you can perform, differs from mine. Everyone possesses a perceived capacity. Similarly, each person has a unique ability to cultivate an enchanting presence.

Yet capacity can grow and strengthen. If you are managing to continually increase your level of success in your profession or chosen pursuit, it's likely you are growing your capacity. However, without a concerted effort to continuously expand your capacity, your growth could level off.

Fortunately, there's uplifting news: capacities are infinitely expandable. This can consequently bolster our ability to grow. Subsequently, a person keen to influence others must strive toward perpetual growth and transformation such that they become an improved version of themselves. Those who aspire to influential status and remarkable allure must commit to the task. "No matter who you are, no matter what you did, no matter where you've come from, you can always change, become a better version of yourself," said Madonna Ciccone. It's a relentless journey of self-transformation, increasing one's worth via conscious enhancement of competence and social aptitudes. Irresistible attractiveness does not materialize without self-awareness, but maintaining optimal personal growth consistently ensures we project our finest version of ourselves to the world.

Developing stronger social skills might mean engaging with people more frequently, participating in discussion groups, fostering positive relationships, venturing into public speaking, developing emotional balance, experimenting with diverse conversation styles, or reading constructive literature. More importantly, advancing yourself also happens when you collaborate closely with others. Collective effort and mutual reliance amplify our capabilities. Our regular interactions teach us extensively. Reflect on your social progression and how you relate to those around you. Which version of yourself do you present for the world to see?

Prioritize Self-Development

"Work on yourself more than you work on your job," Jim Rohn, entrepreneur and author of *How to Obtain Wealth and Happiness,* wisely commented. This proposition made me thoroughly reflect on myself to better grasp the statement's significance. I suggest you also consider the meaning of Jim Rohn's statement. We must invest in self-improvement to enhance our work and ultimately enrich our lives and futures.

Often people dedicate immense effort to their professional roles and neglect their own development. Consequently, they feel overwhelmed and at a standstill in their careers or pursuits. Indeed, some individuals are not even actively engaged in work or a vocation due to a deficiency in skills or knowledge. The quality of our contributions in our professions—or any endeavor—will not improve unless we become more adept. Viktor E. Frankl, Holocaust survivor and author of *Man's Search for Meaning,* observed that "When we are no longer able to change a situation, we are challenged to change ourselves." Hence, self-investment is key to increasing our worth.

This principle holds significant weight because, universally, there is a preference to connect with those who have enriched themselves and, as a result, possess considerable value. It is unlikely anyone would seek out someone with little to contribute. In other words, ***the value you bring to the marketplace determines your placement in the marketplace. The more valuable you are, the more others seek you out because of your expertise and capabilities.***

I urge you to prioritize self-development. Just as you are committed to your professional duties, you also have a personal responsibility to develop yourself. What does this entail? It involves strategizing how to enhance your expertise, capabilities, and experiences.

Reflect on what you require next in your career progression. Which competency should you develop first? In what areas can you improve? What new experiences should you pursue? Consider how you might enhance discipline or time management, for example. Identify behaviors to eliminate or initiate and new habits to adopt. Have you ever pondered these questions?

Self-improvement demands confronting difficult questions, devising a plan of action, and adhering to it. For some, this could mean enrolling in formal education; for others, it could involve cultivating self-discipline for informal learning. Irrespective of the method, everyone has the potential for learning and skill enhancement in their chosen endeavor. If you've decided on a path, commit to mastering the necessary skills to excel and be the best version of yourself within that domain.

Mastering a new skill requires persistent practice until proficiency is achieved. Always remember that your circumstances will only shift when you make personal changes. Elevating your value amplifies your appeal, making you a magnet for those seeking your expertise and abilities to address their challenges.

Exhibit Sportsmanship

Early in my career, I assumed uniformity of behavior across large teams or organizations. I thought things would work well if people would just think the same way and get along. It quickly became apparent that individuals are shaped by their diverse backgrounds, experiences, and beliefs, which influence their perspectives and actions. Everyone views the world through a different lens, leading to varied behaviors, opinions, and decisions. What excites one person may not resonate with another, and what is treasured by someone might be devalued by someone else. Yet for society to function effectively, we must learn to understand and coexist *with* those differences. I now realize that it is more about cooperation than "groupthink." Without widespread cooperation and fellowship, we risk descending into disorder and chaos.

While homogenizing thoughts is neither practical nor conducive to innovation, we are all obligated to express our opinions and ideas respectfully and impartially. The art lies in collaborating with grace, even on an uneven playing field. My observations have led me to understand that those who force their thoughts and plans on others uncooperatively or disrespectfully do not progress far before encountering issues. Conversely, when we act fairly, honestly, decently, truthfully, and with grace, positive outcomes arise. Ultimately, it's about contributing to the collective good rather than focusing solely on personal ego.

Therefore, consider your capacity for sportsmanship. Can you remain gracious in the face of unfavorable odds or differing opinions? What would happen if your opinion was not the final decision? Often it is necessary to take losses with good spirit if it serves the wider interests of society. Refrain from any impulse to undermine others, to disrupt their means of support, or to treat others with disrespect. Uphold the ethical standards of kindness and respect for all. Abigail Van Buren, otherwise known as Dear Abby, once noted, "The best index to a person's character is how they treat people who can't do them any good, and how they treat people who can't fight back." Embrace love for others over animosity. ***Even when you must compete, do so with integrity and*** *let your sportsmanship be evident. That is how you win people to your side.*

Lead Rather Than Follow

Upon encountering this heading, you might have pondered whether it implies a world with only leaders and no followers. This brings to light a significant concept: humans are inherently built not to follow but to lead. Is it possible for everyone to be a leader? Indeed, by harnessing our talents and abilities, we can each lead in our specialized domains. That does not mean you will not look up to anyone or that you will not subject yourself to the direction of your work superiors but that you have unique attributes to contribute as an individual.

Consider the sheep, an animal inherently predisposed to follow. A flock lacks a designated leader because leadership is not an intrinsic trait of sheep; this necessitates the presence of a shepherd for guidance. Hence, being likened to a sheep is hardly a compliment. In contrast, being compared to a lion or an eagle implies strategic prowess and innate leadership capabilities.

What's the takeaway here? Though you can and must follow in certain spheres and at certain times, you are not crafted to simply trail behind others. One may wonder what to do with such a plethora of exceptional leaders around. My suggestion is to learn from their wisdom, engage with their offerings if valuable, or contribute alongside them, rather than merely following. You need to always ask yourself what you can uniquely contribute.

The late Dr. Myles Munroe, leadership consultant and Bahamian evangelist, on many occasions asserted that every person is fashioned to exert dominion over their sphere of influence, indicating that leadership is embedded in our essence. *By dedicating yourself to honing your personal skills and sharing them with the world, you step into a leadership role.* The individuals you serve become your clientele. You can be a luminary in your field, encourage others to find their strengths, and be a patron of other leaders. There is enough room for each of us to flourish.

Every person has a distinct position and mission to fulfill. Letting your authentic self manifest through your dedication to your talents draws people to you. Excelling in your talent manifests your unique appeal. This magnetic quality often explains why talented individuals attract crowds. Think about the talented people you know—musicians, actors, artists, and world leaders—who through their talents continue to draw others in. So what about you? Embrace your calling to lead in your endeavors through what you already possess: your skills and talents. Strive to embody your inherent leadership qualities rather than just follow others.

Moreover, I've observed that effective leaders have a knack for maintaining stability, particularly during tough times. Genuine leaders are well-balanced and strive to be in command of their circumstances. They often strive to remain undisturbed even amid significant challenges. The importance of balance in leadership is undeniable. Unsteady leaders do not inspire or support others effectively, and the inability to manage oneself typically translates into an inability to lead.

Assessing someone's leadership maturity is simple: observe how they reason and act when faced with adversity. Attributes such as blaming, shirking responsibility, giving up, avoiding dialogue, showing partiality, and inflicting consequences on others signal a lack of leadership strength and maturity. True leadership requires composure, self-assurance, and rationality.

Leaders must master the art of staying calm and balanced. If you aspire to lead effectively, mastering self-control and supporting others through equilibrium is crucial. Do not become unsteady when confronted with issues. Keep in mind that others rely on you. Eleanor Roosevelt once stated, "You gain strength, courage, and confidence by each experience in which you stop to look fear in the face... you must do that which you think you cannot."

Actions speak louder than words. Motivational speeches mean little if you fold under pressure. Those influenced by your actions need to see you lead by example. Whether it's your team, friends, family, or colleagues, they expect to see your guidance.

Most importantly, we can lead gracefully, inspiring others around us. To lead gracefully is to possess a conviction of eventual success even in the face of challenges and to offer those around you the opportunity to observe and absorb the grace and respect within you.

Be a Thoughtful Thought Leader

Are you regarded as a source of knowledge and expertise in your professional domain, sought after for insights, mentorship, direction, encouragement, or advice? Do people respect your prowess and contributions, perceiving you as an authority? If so, you embody the qualities of a thought leader. You are perceived as a go-to individual, offering genuine expertise and information.

Thought leaders have significant influence. Engaging with a thought leader in your industry can offer substantial learning opportunities and access to their extensive experience. Nevertheless, thought leadership is not entirely effective without the leader applying depth, mindfulness, and empathy to their intellect. Consider a rocket scientist who, despite immense technical knowledge, fails to develop the necessary interpersonal relationships due to personal shortcomings. "The state of your life is nothing more than a reflection of your state of mind," said Wayne W. Dyer, a renowned author and speaker in the field of self-development and motivation.

Mindful individuals direct their thoughts toward the needs and feelings of others, the nature of their own interpersonal relations, and the consequences of their own actions. They understand that intelligence alone is insufficient; wisdom holds even greater value. Thoughtfulness should complement intellectual leadership. An influential leader exhibits both strength of character and influence. Such leaders ponder meticulously, take time for introspection, display empathy, and avoid impulsive judgments. Thoughtfulness denotes meticulous and considerate deliberation and the careful consideration of various aspects of a matter before initiating action.

People who are strong, courageous, and nurturing are often drawn to leaders who exhibit thoughtfulness. Therefore, a mindful leader naturally attracts those capable of contributing to their personal success. It's no coincidence that thoughtful individuals often achieve great success. Conversely, someone who is intelligent and talented yet struggles to foster positive collaborations or dissuades amiable personalities should reassess their level of thoughtfulness. Strive not only to be a thought leader but a leader who embodies thoughtfulness.

Leading in the Right Way

When individuals describe themselves as results-oriented, it could signify various things. It might indicate they can complete tasks, reach significant achievements, or meet certain objectives. Yet sometimes, this focus on results can lead to disregard for the means, methods, or processes used to achieve the goal or result, or in other words, "the end justifies the means." For some, positive results may justify bypassing rules or pushing employees too hard. Others might even sacrifice personal relationships and health in pursuit of success.

I want to specifically address the tendency to view people as mere resources in the quest for achieving results, often treating them as expendable as numbers on a spreadsheet. The reality is that people are more valuable than the task at hand. Leadership should not be about exploiting individuals like you would exploit an ox with a plow but about developing individuals who enhance society. My guiding principle has always been to create an atmosphere where people feel valued and know they are more important than their output. Good leadership is not about command and control; it is about inspiring positive change in others.

Creating a collaborative work environment makes achieving tasks effortless. *By nurturing and empowering our teams and offering clear guidance, exceptional outcomes naturally follow.* Leading effectively involves lighting the path for others, providing them with the necessary tools and preparation, then allowing them to make the journey on their own. Your appeal and effectiveness as a leader come down to how you exercise your leadership abilities. What does your leadership look like?

CHAPTER 1 SUMMARY

This chapter provided insights into developing a captivating presence that attracts and inspires others, emphasizing the importance of personal growth, graciousness, resilience, and thoughtful leadership. Here are the key lessons from this chapter.

1. Graciousness and courtesy
   - Being gracious and courteous helps build positive relationships and foster trust. Gracious people are kind and forgiving and maintain a positive attitude toward others.
2. Continuous self-improvement
   - Elevating yourself involves continuous self-improvement in such areas as communication, emotional regulation, and patience. This commitment expands your capacity to charm and captivate others.
3. Prioritize self-development
   - Investing in self-improvement is crucial for enhancing your overall worth. This involves identifying areas for growth and committing to mastering new skills.
4. Exhibit sportsmanship
   - Displaying sportsmanship by acting fairly, honestly, and respectfully, even in unfavorable conditions, contributes to positive outcomes and effective collaboration.
5. Lead rather than follow
   - Everyone has the potential to lead in their own domains by harnessing their unique talents and abilities. Leading involves inspiring positive change rather than merely following others.
6. Thoughtful leadership
   - Thought leadership should be complemented by thoughtfulness and involve empathy, careful deliberation, and consideration of others' needs and feelings. This combination attracts capable individuals and leads to greater success.

CHAPTER 1 REFLECTIONS FOR ACTION

It's time to act on what you have learned in this chapter. Kindly read the reflection questions in the following table, and in the space provided, note what actions you will take and when.

	Reflection Questions
1	Rate your graciousness on a scale of one to five, with five being very gracious. Consider ways you could increase your graciousness when interacting with others.
	Notes to self:
2	Consider how much of your day is devoted to your employment versus self-improvement. Are you dedicating sufficient resources to self-improvement? Determine and enumerate three aspects where you could enhance yourself. In what ways would these improvements increase your worth?
	Notes to self:
3	Analyze these aspects of your self-improvement: verbal communication, behavior, and personal ethics. Once you've discovered your weak spots, take proactive steps to enhance them. This may require creating a structured plan or seeking assistance.
	Notes to self:

4	Reflect on your goals and the potential obstacles you might face. Consider solutions to these challenges. If you find yourself close to abandoning an aspiration due to setbacks, think about alternative approaches that might give you a fresh opportunity to succeed.
	Notes to self:
5	Take an objective look at your circumstances. Are there aspects that are burdensome or particularly difficult? List three strategies to proceed despite these challenges. Allow yourself to brainstorm and welcome ideas. Make the conscious decision to not be dominated by hardships. Affirm to yourself that you have the strength to endure.
	Notes to self:
6	Consider your behavior when interacting with others. Are you treating them with fairness and respect? Commit to consistently conducting yourself with integrity and grace. Strive to be someone who is universally recognized for their sportsmanship. Look for opportunities to improve how benevolent you are to those around you.
	Notes to self:

7	Engage in self-assessment to gauge your degree of consideration when addressing problems and interacting with people. Do you consistently act with thoughtfulness? Make a deliberate effort to incorporate thoughtfulness into all aspects of your life. Keep in mind, your actions and emotions have an impact on those around you. Aim to be considerate.
	Notes to self:
8	Evaluate your approach to leadership. Consider if you push people to get results or if they are naturally motivated to exceed expectations when they work with you. Now is the moment for advancement. Regardless of your past performance as a leader, always look for opportunities to further develop your ability to support others in their growth.
	Notes to self:

CHAPTER 2

RECALIBRATE YOUR MINDSET AND ATTITUDE

Success is a state of mind. If you want success, start thinking of yourself as a success.

~ Joyce Brothers ~

We often encounter various challenges that test our resilience and determination. During these times of adversity, our mental strength becomes paramount. This mental strength is determined by the state of the very nucleus of our being, that is, our subconscious mind, which acts as a repository of information from which we form our philosophy, decisions, and actions. Through deliberate effort, we must vigilantly monitor and influence this repository as it determines the outcomes of our lives.

We should realize that setbacks and failures are inevitable, yet they should not define us. Instead, they offer invaluable lessons that propel us toward greater achievements. Attaining greater achievements despite setbacks depends on the state of one's subconscious mind, hence, one's mindset. Meanwhile, recalibrating one's mindset involves embracing the idea that our thoughts determine our destiny. By controlling the information we allow into our minds and aligning our thoughts with our vision for life, we pave paths for personal growth and success.

In this chapter, I intend to elucidate the profound impact our thoughts and attitudes have on our lives. As I delve deeper, I invite you to join me in exploring practical actions that will help you recalibrate your mindset. Together, we will uncover the power of our thoughts, the importance of controlling our thoughts, and the impact of our mindset. Let us arm ourselves with the knowledge that our mindset is the key to unlocking our fullest potential. We must evaluate our thoughts, adopt new perspectives, and remain steadfast in the face of disappointments.

In the next pages, I will share insights and strategies that have personally resonated with me and influenced my journey. From evaluating the content of your subconscious mind to adopting novel approaches to achieve your goals, you will find the tools needed to navigate life's challenges with confidence and optimism. These tools will empower you to command an irresistible presence, making you a personal magnet for those you need on your journey. Remember, the power to change your life lies within your thoughts and attitudes. More importantly, your thoughts and attitudes determine your association and the environment you create around yourself. Let us begin this transformative journey together.

Stand at the Gate of Your Mind

At the core of everything we do is our thought process. Each of us possesses both a conscious and a subconscious mind. To use a personal-computer analogy, the subconscious mind functions like a hard drive, while the conscious mind operates like random access memory, or RAM. The conscious mind, RAM, processes information currently being used by the brain and retrieves data stored in the subconscious mind, the hard drive, during the thinking process. This method, sometimes referred to as meditation, enables individuals to tap into their creativity.

An interesting aspect of the computer analogy is that neither positive nor negative information simply appears in our conscious or subconscious mind. We acquire the information for our conscious thoughts through external means called "senses." Therefore, the conscious mind serves as a gateway for the subconscious mind, passing on external information to be stored within it and imprinting our feelings in it. This creates our beliefs. What is ingrained and reinforced in our subconscious then becomes what we call our mental attitude or mindset. The mindset dictates how we perceive circumstances, respond to situations, and make decisions.

Since the subconscious mind houses our philosophy, worldview, choices, decisions, and actions, it governs all that we do. How does the mind achieve this? Consider when you drive to work along the same route every day. Your mind knows the route so well that you no longer need to consciously navigate. Even when not paying attention, you still make all the necessary turns and arrive at your office. Similarly, think of the countless songs you can sing from memory without actively thinking about them. Most daily decisions are made *unconsciously* through automatic suggestions from our subconscious.

Even when decisions are made *consciously*, we face dilemmas if external information conflicts with the beliefs held in our subconscious. At such times, there is a clash between external information from our conscious mind and automated suggestions from our subconscious. Yet the subconscious mind is so influential, it usually prevails. That's why individuals often reject advice in favor of their own decisions. Essentially, we are automatically governed by our subconscious.

Since the subconscious directs our thoughts and decisions, we must carefully monitor how its contents are formed. You are the guardian of your mind. Nothing enters your subconscious without first passing through your senses: what you see, hear, touch, smell, and taste. The conscious mind receives this information, sorts it, and passes it on for storage. How you handle this information is crucial; you can either reject it or process (think about) it. Eventually, your mindset is shaped by what you have accepted into your thoughts and allowed to settle in your subconscious. You become what you think.

The role of the subconscious is significant because it stores both positive and negative content for future reference. Sometimes termed the "heart," the subconscious must be guarded diligently as it influences our future decisions and actions. This is vital. *Our perception of ourselves and the world around us mirrors who we are internally.* Attracting the right people and opportunities depends on maintaining the right mindset. It is unlikely anyone will become someone they cannot conceive mentally. Ultimately, everyone becomes what they think.

One Thing You Must Not Allow

Have you ever experienced a severe setback? Does it seem like life is knocking you down right now? Life often throws challenges our way, and there is no assurance we won't face difficulties. No one can guarantee failure won't occur. Indeed, life is composed of both successes and failures, along with good and bad times.

I want to clarify that this isn't meant to be pessimistic. Many individuals remain down when they are beaten because they choose not to rise again. Although life presents obstacles and disappointments, giving up because of failure is not an option. You must get up and keep trying, repeatedly. You can't let life's challenges overwhelm you entirely.

Consider it from this perspective. Imagine falling from a height, perhaps a hill. You'll eventually reach a point where you can't descend further. This is the valley. When you're in the valley and refuse to remain there, the only direction left is up. Every valley experience can lead to an uphill journey; the choice is ours to make. You must not allow yourself to stay down.

I have resolved to keep making the effort and to explore different methods until I achieve success. For me, quitting is not an option. What about you? Will you let your problems define you, or will you allow setbacks to keep you down? Yes, real challenges exist, but they are meant to be overcome. We all have the choice to rise above the storms and soar like an eagle.

It is crucial not to become demoralized or feel completely hopeless when you encounter failure. Your capability to navigate life's complexities is essential for becoming the best version of yourself. This overcoming version of yourself must first manifest in your thoughts and attitude though. Your mindset should affirm that there is indeed light at the end of the tunnel.

You can't afford to remain down. Succumbing to failure and resignation doesn't benefit anyone. No one becomes more valuable by accepting failure. As Dale Carnegie said, "Most of the important things in the world have been accomplished by people who have kept on trying when there seemed to be no hope at all." Your ability to rise and claim your space will be visible to those around you. Your resolve to overcome obstacles and weather the storms of life will become a source of hope and inspiration to those who hear your story.

Moreover, rising above difficult situations does not happen by resolve only. We must seek the knowledge we need to succeed in our endeavors. Let us look at this in the next section.

What You Don't Know Won't Work for You

The cost of ignorance is exceedingly high. People expend unnecessary effort when they lack the proper perspective, information, data, ideas, or parameters and end up with little to no results to show for the effort. Ignorance leads to hard work without meaningful outcomes, whereas knowledge enables efficient and effective work. Plato once remarked, "Better to be unborn than untaught, for ignorance is the root of all misfortune."

What investment will you make to achieve success in what you are doing? Often, the price we must pay is acquiring the necessary information. Operating from a foundation of knowledge dispels doubts and uncertainties on our path to achievement.

Knowledge application surpasses mere effort. Before embarking on any task, ask yourself what information is crucial. Do you have the knowledge needed to succeed in your daily activities, job, or profession? Do you know where to find resources that can shield you from ignorance?

What you don't know cannot benefit you. Without acquiring knowledge, you can't expect to reap its benefits. An average adult might read one nonfiction book annually. If you read like an average person, expect average results. This disparity explains why excellence is rare compared to mediocrity. Successful individuals fervently pursue knowledge, seeking insights others overlook.

Fortunately, most information required for success is available through books, podcasts, magazines, videos, and other accessible formats now. All it takes is a commitment to learning. Remember, ignorance won't serve you; it's not virtuous to remain uninformed. You don't know what you don't know.

The knowledge you possess, the actions you take, and your resulting success will attract others. ***People naturally gravitate*** *to those with solutions.* In a world seeking answers, being knowledgeable will draw many to you.

Ditch the Alibis and Forget the Excuses

Why do you behave the way you do? How did you develop your behavior and outlook on life? Every one of us has an underlying reason for our self-expression. None of us developed our personalities by chance. Our thinking patterns—and consequently our worldview, behavior, and responses to life's issues—are shaped by specific influencing systems.

One pertinent question is this: what system shaped you? If you were born into and grew up in a family practicing Islam as a religion, the likelihood of continuing that practice into adulthood is high. Similarly, someone raised in a Christian environment is more likely to be a Christian as an adult. This concept can extend to various facets of our lives, as our backgrounds and experiences profoundly influence our life philosophies.

The systems that shape ones thinking and philosophies can have either positive or negative impacts on life outcomes. Our ideas and beliefs can either empower or hinder our success. For instance, an individual brought up in an oppressive environment may develop low self-esteem.

One thing remains certain: irrespective of the systems that influenced us, everyone is responsible for their own behavior and life outcomes. Self-awareness is required to reassess your background influences, thoughts, and philosophies to identify what should be unlearned and relearned. We all have opportunities to reconsider our beliefs and philosophies. If you are dissatisfied with how you were shaped, now that you recognize it, take action. **Unlearn and relearn to align your philosophies with the** *future you envision.* As Bruce Lee said, "Absorb what is useful. Discard what is not. Add what is uniquely your own."

People often justify their lack of success with excuses, or they blame others for actions or inactions. A typical example is a forty-year-old stating, "My father didn't send me to school, and that's why I lack formal education." Should we not ask, "Now that you know that, what are you doing about it?" Seldom do we hear individuals taking responsibility for their life outcomes, regardless of what they might be.

Everyone has opportunities. While it's true that opportunities are not equal, we all possess them. One commonality among us all is the ability to visualize—to envision. What fundamentally differentiates the rich and the poor, the successful and the mediocre, is their mindset. Everyone can think, but our thought processes vary.

Consider a lion waking up with this resolve: "I will go out there and eat the biggest elephant for lunch," despite the lesser strength and possibly lesser intelligence than the elephant. On the other hand, the elephant laments, "What a terrible day. I will be preyed upon by lions," as it forgets its ability to trample them. Is everyone not accountable for their life outcomes?

Embracing full self-responsibility for our life outcomes marks the transition from immaturity to maturity. Persisting in blame games depletes the willpower to progress. As Joyce Brothers, a psychologist, said, "Success is a state of mind. If you want success, start thinking of yourself as a success."

Abandon alibis and excuses to cultivate a success-oriented mindset. Remember, we all share this trait: the ability to think. How do you utilize your thinking?

You Had It Neither Before nor After

Throughout my life, I have consistently pursued what I desired. I would decide on my goals and strive to achieve them with relentless effort. Inevitably, this journey involved numerous successes and failures. Whenever I fell short of my objectives, I felt disappointment but also found the resilience to try again. Indeed, I encountered many setbacks and obstacles along the way.

My experiences have taught me that true success in life is like a tapestry woven from both victories and defeats. Sometimes we succeed, other times we do not. The path to success is rarely straightforward. What sustains me is the understanding that worrying over missed opportunities is futile. If I aim for something and fail to achieve it, my anxiety over the outcome serves no purpose. After all, I did not possess my objective before attempting to attain it, and I still do not have it afterward.

For instance, if you apply for a job and do not get hired after the interviews, you have lost nothing. You were without the job before you applied and remained so afterward. The benefit lies in the experience gained during the process.

Before becoming too discouraged by unachieved goals or missed opportunities, consider that your effort was worthwhile. Instead of dwelling on what was not attained, use that energy to prepare for a better attempt next time. Each failure teaches us valuable lessons and propels us forward. This echoes Martin Luther King Jr.'s poignant words: "We must accept finite disappointment, but never lose infinite hope."

Whatever your aspirations, one effective strategy for handling disappointments is to remember that you neither had the goal before nor after your attempt. A positive attitude can provide the strength to keep moving forward; it is fundamentally about mindset.

Accepting that things may not always turn out as planned, at least not every time, makes you a stronger individual. This mindset equips you to face challenges with resilience. Learning to manage disappointments positions you to become a source of encouragement and inspiration for others. Your story of resilience in overcoming life's issues will draw people in, attracting them because they want to benefit from your experience. In turn, some of these people will open influential doors for you.

It's All Bright and Beautiful

No matter how much effort we put in, our understanding of the world will always be limited compared to what remains unknown. You could devote your entire life to seeking answers and striving to know all, yet you will encounter limitations in your knowledge.

One key source of our frustration with life is our incomplete grasp of both our own circumstances and those of others around us. We experience both positives and negatives in ways that often defy explanation. How do you make sense of some individuals being born into privilege while others are born into scarcity? Why are people's fortunes so unequal? Why do adverse events impact good people, and why do the wicked seem to prosper? Why does opportunity knock for some and not others?

Do I hold the answers? Certainly not. But one thing is clear: what happens to us is merely a minuscule part of the broader spectrum of events occurring worldwide. Moreover, our experiences may resonate with those of people elsewhere, meaning that we are not always alone in our experiences. This realization leads me to believe that we can adjust our outlook on life. When confronted with uncertainty, we have the choice to focus on the positive aspects rather than the negative. We can focus on what we have rather than what we don't have. Accept that we can't know everything and focus on what we've learned and what we can continue to learn.

Regardless of how scorching a day might be, there will always be some shade providing relief. We must opt to see the beauty and brightness in life. Staying optimistic has its benefits. Beautiful outcomes arise from cultivating a positive mindset. As Charles Dickens noted, "The sun himself is weak when he first rises, and gathers strength and courage as the day gets on." Rather than dwelling on what we don't understand, we should trust and accept that everything holds potential beauty. This doesn't mean ignoring our experiences but acknowledging that we can influence our perspective on them.

A pertinent question to ask yourself is what is your overall perspective on life? Do you view things through an optimistic or pessimistic lens? Your attitude and mindset fundamentally shape your happiness and satisfaction. It's not merely our possessions or achievements, nor the successes or failures we encounter, that dictate our fulfillment; it's our thoughts about these experiences.

Before concluding that no one appreciates you and everything is against you, take a moment to reflect on your own outlook. I've observed that ***individuals who maintain a positive view of life and believe deeply in the power of positivity tend to attract remarkable people.*** Individuals with a mastery of personal magnetism through their positive outlook on life are thus bestowed with an irresistible charm.

You May Take It or Leave It

We live in a time where everyone seems to possess their own version of the truth. The boundary between right and wrong is becoming increasingly unclear. The concept of "truth" now varies depending on one's viewpoint. Being correct or incorrect now hinges on multiple factors. It's as if we've lost our compass, causing us to lose our sense of direction, our true north.

The effects of this relative truth can be observed and felt everywhere: at work, at home, in legislative centers. Yet, we need to establish something clearly: even if someone faces west and calls it north, the actual position of north remains unchanged. Are there certain aspects of life we all must continue to learn, fundamental principles that could lead us to what is truly accurate?

For instance, most people agree with the scientific principles that laid the foundation for many modern inventions. Disagreeing with the law of gravity, for example, has obvious consequences. Principles are true, and when applied correctly, they yield successful outcomes. Thus, there are fundamental principles that guide success in areas such as finance, marriage, health, business, leadership, and every other aspect of life.

Crucially, we do not create fundamental principles (truths) based on our own interpretations. We learn or discover these principles. Just because something feels right to you, or you are convinced and sincere about something, does not make it true or correct. You can only know something is right or true when you test it against established principles. This implies that anyone can be sincerely wrong but feel like they're sincerely right.

What principles guide your actions? Where does your compass point? Regardless of your stance, what is true remains true. W. Clement Stone said, "Truth will always be truth, regardless of lack of understanding, disbelief or ignorance." Your attitude toward the truth significantly impacts your journey toward success. Instead of creating your own version of the truth based on feelings and desires, why not earnestly seek out what *is* true and live by it? Remember, at the core of everything we do and what we become is our mindset. It is your responsibility to become a person of integrity and authenticity.

See the Vessel from the Inside

Most individuals are captivated by what is immediately visible. We often judge a book by its cover without delving deeper into its contents. Decisions are commonly made based on surface-level observations, neglecting the unseen aspects. Yet the most valuable treasures are often hidden.

If diamonds were as common as river stones readily found on the ground, everyone would use them to construct their homes. However, diamonds are rare and buried deep; they require effort to uncover. Similarly, exceptional and resourceful people are not easily found. How do you perceive others? Is it through their outward appearance and momentary impressions, or do you consider who they truly are inside?

Each of us resembles a full vessel that has both an exterior facade and inner substance. No one fully understands what lies within until it is shown. It is essential to give others the opportunity to showcase their true selves. Unfortunately, we often assess people only on superficial traits such as history and charisma, overlooking their potential and true capabilities. This is akin to a job interview where one's talents and abilities are evaluated in just an hour. The genuine person needs to be discovered from within, and that takes time. When we don't provide individuals this chance, their true nature remains concealed.

Appearances can be deceptive. Cease making judgments about others based solely on visible traits; instead, focus on their inherent potential and capabilities. Many people carry more potential than is evident at first glance. Aim to perceive beyond the exterior. Just as you wish for others to recognize your own gifts and abilities, seek to understand the strengths and potential of those around you.

Moreover, we must acknowledge that great individuals draw other great individuals to them, just as like attracts like. You are likely to attract the type of person you embody. If you aspire to connect with valuable individuals who possess excellent internal qualities to support your goals or collaborate with you, strive first to become a person of substance and worth. This is a key secret known by those who exemplify mastery in personal magnetism.

Just Do It and Forget the Payback

When I was about ten years old, my dad encouraged me to join a boys' group called the Royal Ambassadors at the Baptist Church. One of my initial tasks as a new member was to engage in community service without expecting any reward or benefit in return.

This was an excellent way to teach young people the value of service! This principle has guided me throughout my life. I have learned to support, give, and help others sincerely, without anticipating anything in return. Have I been able to assist everyone? No, but I have practiced this principle whenever possible.

When you are supporting friends, family, or colleagues, when you offer gifts, money, or materials, do you do it for a potential benefit or to earn goodwill? While it is acceptable to pay it forward with future benefits in mind, I challenge you to elevate your mindset to a higher level of service: giving without expecting anything in return and serving without the hope of a reward now or later. Charles Dickens once said, "There were two classes of charitable people: one, the people who did a little and made a great deal of noise; the other, the people who did a great deal and made no noise at all." Which category do you fall into?

Here is my challenge to you: find someone to support, uplift, provide for, patronize, promote, or work for without expecting anything in return. Is there a genuine need among your friends, family, colleagues, or community? How can you meet that need selflessly? Can you give freely and wholeheartedly without ulterior motives?

Sometimes we must aid those who are unable to repay us even if they wish to. Look around carefully; there are numerous opportunities to be a source of help, support, patronage, and blessings to others. Act and forget about repayment. Give freely; give unconditionally. It's not complicated; a person who gives freely often has many friends. Our ability to attract people also depends on generosity born of genuine love for humanity.

A Healthy Dose of Pride

We were discussing self-confidence in a virtual room a while ago when someone asked about the difference between confidence and arrogance. Arrogance makes a person self-centered, egotistical, and proud. In contrast, self-confidence involves having faith and trust in one's abilities.

Here's a quick question: is there not a fine line between pride and self-confidence? It seems self-confidence balanced with humility makes a person appear decent. Highly self-confident individuals with many talents and skills should keep humility close. Being overly self-confident without humility is indistinguishable from arrogance.

This is why we must self-examine to understand how others perceive us. Why is this important? An arrogant person will struggle to earn the trust and commitment of others, while the truly self-confident will attract others. No one really wants to follow an egotistical individual. Showcasing talents and gifts without humility does significant harm to oneself.

Sometimes, it may even be about others' perceptions. Unfortunately, you cannot control what others think of you, only how you behave. Balancing self-confidence with ample humility is everyone's responsibility. Be confident, but do not boast.

Does humility mean lowering your head and losing your self-esteem and worth? Absolutely not. Humility is about modesty. Rick Warren reminded us that "Humility is not thinking less of yourself, it's thinking of yourself less." It involves not thinking too highly of oneself but allowing others to praise us. A balance of humility and self-confidence is found in those who have mastered personal magnetism.

CHAPTER 2 SUMMARY

Reflecting on the lessons learned from this chapter, it is evident that the path to personal growth and a meaningful life is intricately tied to our mindset and actions. Below are the key takeaways that encapsulate the essence of our conversation, each offering a profound insight into nurturing a life of purpose, humility, and generosity.

1. Stand at the gate of your mind
   - Your conscious mind acts as a gateway to your subconscious. Guarding this gateway ensures that only beneficial information shapes your mindset and decisions.
2. One thing you must not allow
   - Life inevitably presents challenges and setbacks. It is essential to rise after every fall and view failures as opportunities to learn and grow. Do not stay down.
3. What you don't know won't work for you

- Ignorance leads to wasted effort, while knowledge empowers effective action. Pursuing knowledge diligently is crucial for success.
4. Ditch the alibis and forget the excuses
    - Everyone is responsible for their own life outcomes. Instead of making excuses, take responsibility and adjust your mindset and actions to align with your goals.
5. You had it neither before nor after
    - Worrying over missed opportunities is pointless. Focus on the lessons learned from failed attempts and prepare better for future endeavors.
6. It's all bright and beautiful
    - An optimistic outlook helps you navigate life's uncertainties. Choosing to see the positive aspects can significantly improve your overall perspective and satisfaction.
7. You may take it or leave it
    - Principles remain true regardless of personal beliefs. Seek out and adhere to fundamental truths to guide your actions and decisions.
8. See the vessel from the inside
    - True value and potential are often hidden beneath the surface. Strive to understand the intrinsic qualities of others and yourself.
9. Just do it and forget the payback
    - Engage in acts of service without expecting anything in return. Genuine generosity fosters goodwill and attracts positive relationships.
10. A healthy dose of pride
    - Balance self-confidence with humility. This combination earns trust and respect, distinguishing you from being arrogant.

CHAPTER 2 REFLECTIONS FOR ACTION

It's time to act on what you have learned in this chapter. Kindly read the reflection questions in the following table, and in the space provided, note what actions you will take and when.

	Reflection Questions
1	Do your thoughts match your life's vision? Assess your thoughts to uncover the nature of your subconscious mind. Be deliberate about managing the external information you let into your mind.
	Notes to self:
2	Are you facing setbacks? Resolve to persist and triumph; don't give up. For the next week, remind yourself daily, "I know I can succeed. I am on the path to success. I am capable."
	Notes to self:
3	Consider your personal history and experiences. How have they impacted your perspectives, convictions, and guiding principles? Identify the notions or beliefs you must unlearn. What new insights or knowledge are necessary to positively shape your worldview? How can you continuously immerse yourself in an environment conducive to positive growth?

	Notes to self:
4	Be genuine in your self-reflection. Are you attributing your current situation to someone else? Consider how you can shift from this mindset to taking complete responsibility for all your future outcomes.
	Notes to self:
5	Reflect on how you dealt with previous setbacks on your path to achievement. What lessons did you take away? What could you improve next time? How can you better prepare yourself for opportunities superior to the ones you missed? List three action items and then implement them.
	Notes to self:
6	Reflect on your thinking patterns. Do you often lean toward negativity? Do you have faith that life can be positive and full of beauty? It might be necessary to persuade yourself of this possibility, and gradually, you will start to notice beautiful experiences.
	Notes to self:

7	Have you ever been in a scenario where your capabilities were judged by someone who didn't truly know you? How did that make you feel? Reflect on how you assess others. Consider if there is someone who deserves an opportunity from you. Give that person a chance to prove themselves.
	Notes to self:
8	Reflect on your motivations and habits. Why do you help or give to others? Identify someone whose cause you can support or assist. Reach out to them, learn what they need, then offer your help generously.
	Notes to self:
9	Consider how you can enhance your humility while keeping your self-confidence intact. Allow three to five people who know you well to give their feedback. Request that they rate you on a scale of pride versus humility and then assess the results.
	Notes to self:

CHAPTER 3

EXUDE SELF-BELIEF AND CONFIDENCE

If you want to improve your self-worth, stop giving other people the calculator.

~ Tim Fargo ~

Pursuing personal and professional growth is an important endeavor for each of us. Confidence and self-belief are vital requirements in this endeavor. These twin pillars, crucial for realizing our full potential, serve as part of the foundation upon which we build our dreams and aspirations, as well as an inviting and respectable personality.

As I navigate life, I understand that confidence is not merely an external facade but a deep-seated belief in one's abilities and worth. It is this inner conviction that distinguishes leaders from followers and shapes how others perceive and respond to us. Self-confidence can be likened to the commanding presence of the lion—the undisputed king of the jungle—not because of its size or intelligence, but because of its unwavering belief in its supremacy.

In my quest to cultivate these indispensable qualities of confidence and self-belief, I have encountered numerous barriers, from societal expectations to personal setbacks. Yet I have learned that overcoming these obstacles is essential for one's unique talents and abilities to flourish. Embracing authenticity and having the courage to break free from conformity has been a transformative aspect of my journey, guiding me toward a life led by personal conviction rather than external validation.

The journey toward self-belief and confidence is an ongoing endeavor. It is a continuous process of self-improvement and growth. It is a path that requires a gentle yet firm approach to communication, recognizing the power our words hold in building or breaking confidence, both in ourselves and others. This understanding drives me to reflect on my experiences and share insights that might empower others to take control of their destinies.

In this chapter, I will present what I have learned: a comprehensive understanding of what it truly means to believe in oneself. These lessons remind us that we are all capable, provided we cultivate a strong sense of self and a courageous spirit.

As I delve into this series of lessons, I aim to offer thoughtful reflections and practical advice on developing self-belief and confidence. By doing so, I hope to inspire you to embark on your journey toward unlocking your full potential and making meaningful contributions to the world. If you are already advanced in the journey of success, I hope you can continue to grow on the path of self-belief and confidence. This path is both challenging and rewarding and lies at the heart of our personal and professional success.

The pursuit of self-belief and confidence is not merely a goal but a lifelong journey. It is a journey that requires dedication, introspection, and an unwavering commitment to growth. Self-belief and confidence are major factors in the development of a magnetic personality. Let us start to unwrap this chapter by discussing what it means to become confident.

Become Confident

Have you ever struggled during a speech because you became nervous and couldn't calm yourself due to stage fright? Often, anxiety and a lack of self-confidence rob us of the outstanding performance we envisioned during our preparation.

Consider this: life can resemble a stage performance. An actor prepares thoroughly before going on stage but must be composed and confident to deliver an excellent performance. Similarly, in striving for major achievements in life, we must prepare diligently while also developing confidence and belief in our ability to succeed.

Your dreams are valid, and your aspirations are genuine. Don't let a lack of self-confidence hinder your success. Cultivate strong feelings, deep faith, and personal conviction regarding your endeavors.

If you don't believe in the legitimacy of your dreams and your capability to succeed, others will have no reason to believe in you either. As Tim Fargo, author of *Claimants, Lies and Videotape*, said, "If you want to improve your self-worth, stop giving other people the calculator." When striving to become your best self, develop a sense of certainty and an appreciation for your unique qualities and abilities to achieve your dreams.

Why is the lion considered the king of the jungle? The lion isn't the largest or the smartest animal, yet it confidently believes it can defeat any other creature. Confidence is noticeable to those observing you. Your hesitation and self-doubt will be apparent to others.

Individuals who strongly believe in their pursuits and are confident about succeeding possess an undeniable magnetism. People naturally gravitate toward confident individuals and leaders.

A firm belief in your mission will attract those who will support you even before tangible results appear.

It's time to nurture a profound belief in yourself, an assurance that you can achieve what you aspire to. Trust that your dreams are real, move forward with confident assurance, and do not let anything or anyone stand in your way. Progress with confidence and notice how it enhances your personal allure.

Go Wherever Your Talent Takes You

I've noticed that many people have reasons not to move, try something new, or embark on a new adventure. Although some might be open to small changes, most of us dislike major disruptions, especially when we've been somewhat successful. It appears we settle into a certain social and economic state and stop considering significant shifts. We call this "stability," but often it's just a form of complacency. Everyone aims for this so-called stability, which usually means settling for something much less than our true potential.

We begin with big ambitions and strong drive, but once we achieve a certain level, we often plateau. We end up in situations that don't fully utilize our abilities, and as a result, most people do much less than they are capable of.

Through my interactions with many people, I've learned that we all have multiple aspirations. Many people possess a combination of dreams and untapped talents but are unwilling to take the necessary steps. We settle into routines and resist disrupting them. This mindset leads many to reach the end of their lives without realizing their full potential or achieving their purpose, which often results in regret. There is a time for everything, and once one misses opportunities, it becomes difficult to regain lost time. Therefore, it's crucial to act when the opportunity arises.

I urge you to follow where your talent leads. Do you feel you have more to offer? Are you not reaching your full potential? Is your environment limiting you? Have you settled into situations that make it hard to progress? It's time to leave your comfort zone and confront complacency. Break free from limiting thoughts and try what you thought you couldn't do.

Everyone has a purpose in life. Your gifts and talents are pointers to your purpose and your mission. Don't let current comforts deprive the world of your valuable contributions or prevent you from finding personal fulfillment. If you need to make changes to complete your mission, do it. As Nelson Mandela famously said, "There is no passion to be found playing small—in settling for a life that is less than the one you are capable of living." So, why settle for less? Follow where your talent leads, and in doing so, you'll greatly benefit humanity.

Don't Fit into Anyone's Mold

We exist in a world where people, particularly those with influence over us, expect certain behaviors and actions and conformity. It often feels like others impose their expectations on us, and they may not align with our self-expectations. The resulting pressure leads to the expectation that we become someone we are not.

Our societies are structured to shape our thinking in specific ways through education, work, media, and other influences. These societal constructs often dictate how we perceive ourselves. Unfortunately, those who deviate from these norms may face unpopularity or even punishment for not conforming. However, this forced conformity is frequently why individuals feel unhappy, unfulfilled, and discontented.

The explanation is straightforward. We all possess inherent gifts and talents, and our aspirations should typically align with these natural abilities. Regrettably, many people can't fully express themselves or achieve their dreams because they strive to meet others' expectations. They conform to imposed molds, driven by external dictates. Until we break free from this conformity, true happiness and fulfillment will elude us.

Moreover, the act of conforming and following the crowd signals internal confusion. Many have been misled to believe false narratives about themselves, and that impacts their mental state. Nathaniel Hawthorne aptly noted, "No one man for any considerable period can wear one face to himself, and another to the multitude, without finally getting bewildered as to which may be the true." Conformity can lead to low self-esteem and losing one's sense of personal identity.

It's imperative to start thinking independently and living intentionally, even if it means opposing majority views. I prioritize authenticity over conformity. My choice is to remain true to myself rather than succumbing to external pressures. What about you? Will you let others' opinions shape your life, or will you chart your own course?

Those who live authentically experience joy and fulfillment throughout their lives. Self-belief and confidence in your abilities pave the way to doing what truly matters to you, leading you to happiness. Conversely, pretending leads to frustration, failure, and eventual dissatisfaction.

I have chosen to pursue my true passions and aim to improve continually. How about you? Avoid fitting into anyone's mold. Instead, embrace an authentic life that attracts both people and opportunities, guiding you to ultimate fulfillment.

You Can Be Better Than Your Best

My daughter and I often have engaging discussions whenever she shows me her exam scores. There have been occasions when she scored twenty-four out of twenty-five, and I responded with, "Where did that one missing mark go?" It's a light-hearted remark. She knows I appreciate her performance because I tell her so, but I also remind her that she could capture the missing mark in the next test.

When I hear someone say, "I tried my best," I see it as an opportunity to remind them they can surpass even their strongest efforts. Henry Ford put it this way: "There is no man living who isn't capable of doing more than he thinks he can do." Everyone needs to remember that the metaphorically largest room in the world is the room for improvement.

One major barrier to progress is our mental limitations. Often, we perceive ourselves as confronting a brick wall or reaching a dead end. In those moments, we might say, "There is nothing else I can do," and give up. Other times, after achieving some success, we settle because we believe we've given our all. This sense of satisfaction can deter further achievements. We may rest on our laurels, thinking we've done our utmost when substantial room for growth still exists.

I deeply admire individuals dedicated to lifelong self-improvement, who view success not as a destination but as a continual journey. I've never met anyone committed to relentless self-enhancement who has lagged. Most of the exceptionally successful people I know are devoted to constant personal development and maintain their drive even into old age.

Whenever we stop thinking, it seems like there's nothing more we can do, particularly when faced with challenges. The reason we can't envision doing more is that we stopped contemplating innovative solutions. Regardless of how far you think you've stretched yourself, there's always room for further improvement.

Do you feel you've done your best in your current situation? Try engaging your mind further, and you'll begin to see new opportunities and possibilities. This recalls Ronald Reagan's words: "There are no constraints on the human mind, no walls around the human spirit, no barriers to our progress except those we ourselves erect." Maintaining a mindset that you can always surpass your best will help you stay ahead in any endeavor and in life.

Secure the Courage To Succeed

I have yet to see anyone accomplish something great without courage. Courage is a skill; it's the ability to face challenges or difficulties. It's also the resilience to endure tough times without giving up.

In life, we encounter numerous challenges. We deal with difficult situations at work, home, and various other places. Some struggles involve decision-making while others relate to interacting with people. We push against barriers as we strive toward success. The winds of change require us to stand firm and face situations head-on. Regardless of the circumstances, we all need courage to succeed.

You might wonder: how can I develop courage? Well, courage isn't something that can be given to you. It's an attitude that must be cultivated personally. Although encouragement from others can help, one must learn to embrace courage internally. Being courageous improves with practice. Our level of courage is tested by difficulties and challenges. If you shy away in the face of opposition, lack, setbacks, pain, or obstacles, it may be time to evaluate your courage level. Building courage helps us weather storms. It enables you to remain standing when everything suggests you should fall.

Regardless of your current situation at home, work, or in your community or society, you need courage. You need courage to take that leap. You need courage to overcome challenges. You need courage to make progress and resolve relationship issues. You need courage to excel at your job.

In fact, we all need courage to navigate the complexities of our world. As times change, so must our courage to adapt. One good thing about courage is that it drives us to take positive actions, which helps us stay on top of situations. "Inaction breeds doubt and fear. Action breeds confidence and courage. If you want to conquer fear, do not sit at home and think about it. Go out and get busy," said Dale Carnegie.

The world needs more courageous individuals and leaders. Don't you agree? *Courageous people attract significant attention and respect.* They have mastered personal magnetism. People naturally follow those who dare to pursue their goals. Do not let any situation weigh you down. Do not allow anyone to belittle you. Embrace the courage to rise above and to keep moving forward.

The Real Reason to Do Anything

Sometimes when I see people put in extraordinary effort to accomplish something significant, I often wonder what their source of motivation and energy is. It could be team members who go above and beyond to ensure tasks are completed correctly and satisfactorily or single parents who work during the day and go to school at night or anyone else who gives more than their best.

Those who give their best and selflessly contribute to progress are always inspiring.

One insight I've gained is that everyone has a reason for what they do. While some act out of personal and selfish motivations, I've also witnessed individuals doing impressive things without expecting anything in return. I've realized that the true reason anyone does anything often stems from a genuine connection and mutual respect. When we have real bonds with others, it's easier to step up and give our best.

The importance of relationships, especially those grounded in trust, cannot be overstated. People will go to great lengths to achieve remarkable things for those they truly care about. In these situations, the motivation lies not in the task itself but in the relationship.

Here's a quick test: have you ever done something good for someone just because you liked them, even though you wouldn't have done it for someone else? That's exactly what I mean. The real reason for our actions often comes from love for another person. Otherwise, we might act for selfish reasons.

Consider how much your team, coworkers, or family could accomplish if there were true connections among its members. People flourish and make meaningful contributions when working with those they love and care about. It's crucial for any leader to build relationships, respect, and trust within their team. Relationships give people a reason to do things for others.

Many aspire to be remarkable but are unwilling to go the extra mile for others. They haven't discovered the true reason for their actions. Sometimes, the connection and love we share with others works wonders. We've all seen people bend rules, risk their lives, abdicate positions, and sacrifice everything for the sake of love. This recalls George Eliot's question: "What do we live for, if it is not to make life less difficult for each other?"

I conclude that the true reason to act selflessly lies in having a loving heart. Those who master personal magnetism and seek authentic relationships have the potential to achieve extraordinary things. Likewise, those genuinely interested in solving problems for others, those motivated by sincere care, are the ones who create solutions. Do you possess the true reason to accomplish remarkable things?

Stop Being Realistic

What came to your mind when you first saw the title of this section? Let's be honest. Extreme realism is actually a form of pessimism. What do I mean by that? Consider this: how often have you heard people say, "I am just being realistic," when they really mean, "I don't believe it is possible"?

If you see a tall, steep mountain in front of you, you might think it's realistic that you cannot climb it. Many of us think exactly that. We exaggerate our challenges under the guise of being realistic and then wonder why we aren't accomplishing much or making any changes. We give our problems power and then complain that they persist.

While life's facts cannot be denied—both positive and negative things happen—we cannot focus solely on those facts without using our potential to change and improve our situations. What you label things as will define their existence. What you believe to be your reality will turn into your experience. This isn't about superstition; it's not even about manifestation, as powerful as that is. As I mentioned earlier, when someone says there's nothing more they can do, it means they've stopped thinking. There is always an additional action one can take.

Do not let your current situation, life's facts, and challenges determine your future. Despite the facts, you must believe that better and greater things can happen. It's true that those who expect nothing cannot be disappointed. However, it's equally true that those who expect nothing make no effort, achieve nothing, and become nothing.

True reality is self-created. Instead of empowering our problems, we can choose to change our situations through self-belief and confidence. Tony Robbins said, "What we can or cannot do, what we consider possible or impossible, is rarely a function of our true capability. It is more likely a function of our beliefs about who we are." We won't be able to change our circumstances until we change our mindset and embrace transformation.

Here's how it works. As soon as you convince yourself that things can be different despite your current situation, experiences, or problems—the facts—your mind will start spotting possible solutions. You'll see how things can change and will identify what you can do to make that change happen. Stop being so realistic and start acting and speaking in ways that align with your desired outcomes. When you become the architect of your own destiny, others will recognize and admire your greatness.

Let Your Tongue Be Gentle

I've heard people say that vulgar language is used because of a limited vocabulary. This may or may not be true. I've encountered many well-educated individuals who still opt to use offensive language. It ultimately comes down to choices: our word choices. Developing our everyday language takes considerable time. We do not speak most of the words we frequently use by accident. We learn them over time, often unconsciously, through exposure to different people, media, and interactions.

A troubling aspect of language use is speaking without kindness, using harsh words that can deeply hurt someone else.

Speaking in a hurtful manner does not reflect self-confidence; it often damages someone else's self-esteem. The way we use words is a clear sign of our maturity level. Emotionally stable individuals choose their words carefully, naturally speaking in a modest and respectful manner. This doesn't mean being untruthful but rather communicating the truth in a nonoffensive way.

There is no virtue in hurting others with our words, making disparaging remarks, or using harsh expressions to discuss matters. Once spoken, words cannot be taken back, and we are all responsible for how we affect others with our speech. I chose to address this topic while discussing self-belief and confidence because as we aim to improve ourselves, we also have a responsibility to help others grow. Our words significantly impact other people's confidence, particularly when dealing with younger generations and children. Those whose self-esteem has been harmed since childhood often struggle in life. Let your words come from a place of care and positivity.

A gentle tongue brings about positive change. I've seen calm and thoughtful words transform minds and open doors that were previously closed. The Book of Proverbs 25:15 says, "By patience and a calm spirit, a ruler may be persuaded, and a soft and gentle tongue breaks the bone [of resistance]."

This is a call to tenderness; I encourage us to use our words more mindfully. Even when faced with unkind speech, we can set an example with our gentle responses. It may be challenging, but it is something we can all strive to improve upon.

Interestingly, your words reflect what is in your heart. They reveal whether you possess self-belief and confidence. Your ability to succeed is evident in your speech. Let your heart be filled with gentleness, self-belief, and confidence, and your words will follow. Speak kindly and let your words align with your aspirations for success.

CHAPTER 3 SUMMARY

Self-belief and confidence, while often challenged by societal expectations and personal setbacks, are essential for personal and professional growth. Embracing authenticity and fostering a belief in one's unique abilities lead to overcoming obstacles and achieving one's true potential. Cultivating courage and confidence, and adopting a mindset of continual growth, facilitates remarkable achievements and personal satisfaction. The key lessons in this chapter include the following:

1. Confidence is an internal belief in one's abilities and worth. It is essential for overcoming obstacles and achieving personal and professional growth.
2. Confidence is noticeable to others, and those who strongly believe in their pursuits naturally attract support. Developing self-belief and confidence enhances personal magnetism.
3. Many people settle for stability, but this often leads to complacency and unfulfilled potential. It is crucial to expand upon one's talents and abilities and make necessary changes to achieve personal fulfillment and benefit humanity.
4. Societal expectations often pressure individuals to conform, leading to a loss of personal identity and unhappiness. Authenticity and self-belief are key to achieving true happiness and fulfillment.
5. There is always room for improvement, even when one has done their best. Embracing a mindset of continual growth helps individuals move ahead in any endeavor.
6. Courage is essential for overcoming challenges and achieving success. It is a skill that must be cultivated personally and is crucial for navigating life's complexities.

7. Building genuine connections and relationships motivates one to achieve remarkable things. True bonds and mutual respect inspire people to go the extra mile for others.
8. Extreme realism often disguises pessimism, which limits one's potential. Believing in the possibility of change and acting accordingly transforms one's reality and leads to success.
9. Using gentle and kind language reflects emotional maturity and self-confidence. Thoughtful and positive speech can bring about significant changes and help others grow.

CHAPTER 3 REFLECTIONS FOR ACTION

It's time to act on what you have learned in this chapter. Kindly read the reflection questions in the following table, and in the space provided, note what actions you will take and when.

	Reflection Questions
1	How do you perceive self-confidence? Reflect on a specific area in your life where you've lacked confidence. Commit to addressing this aspect with newfound confidence.
	Notes to self:
2	Identify one to three obstacles or situations currently hindering you from achieving what you know you can and truly want to accomplish. Consider what actions you can take to address these factors. Commit to making the needed changes and progressing. Encourage yourself to believe that you can make this move and allow nothing to impede your progress.

	Notes to self:
3	Are you on the verge of giving up after feeling like you've tried everything? Or are you perhaps settling into a comfort zone? Take a moment to reconsider and find one additional action you can take. Make plans to pursue this identified action. In addition, list three areas where you could enhance your career, business, or chosen endeavor. Then, proceed to implement those improvements.
	Notes to self:
4	Identify one area where you need to confront fear or difficulty. Decide on your plan of action and commit fully to it. As you work toward your goals, visualize what success looks like. Establish your objective and muster the courage to begin and complete it.
	Notes to self:
5	Assess your relationships. Are they robust enough? Aim to cultivate healthy connections whenever you can. Form bonds with others so that influencing each other becomes more attainable. Moreover, do you truly care for others? This week, seek out someone to assist or support.

	Notes to self:
6	Evaluate your mindset. Are you often so pragmatic that it hinders your ability to view situations from different perspectives? Do you frequently declare, "I'm just being realistic"? Analyze your current circumstances and identify the facts. Next, establish where you aspire to be and have confidence in your capacity to reach that destination. Take actions based on your beliefs and maintain forward momentum.
	Notes to self:
7	Reevaluate your vocabulary. Identify the words you need to remove and determine suitable alternatives. Begin incorporating these new words into your daily practice. Commit to using language that is both gracious and considerate. Ensure that your speech uplifts others rather than diminishes them. If needed, alter the environment and media you engage with.
	Notes to self:

CHAPTER 4

USE THE POWER OF PRESENCE TO BUILD MEANINGFUL CONNECTIONS

No one can whistle a symphony. It takes a whole orchestra to play it.

~ H.E. Luccock ~

Our networks and relationships have a profound impact on our lives. The people we surround ourselves with play a significant role in shaping our experiences. It's fascinating how, at different points in our lives, we encounter individuals who leave a lasting impression on us. It may be that they offered support or companionship when we needed it the most.

Showing up for others is a powerful thing. There's a saying that resonates deeply with me: "A friend in need is a friend indeed." This sentiment underscores the importance of being present for those who matter to us, especially during their most challenging times. It's not necessarily about doing big things for people but about the genuine intention behind our actions. Whether it is attending a friend's celebration, offering a helping hand during a crisis, or simply being there to listen, these acts of kindness create a ripple effect of positivity and fulfillment.

I've observed that true friendships and connections are tested during difficult times. It is easy to be surrounded by people during moments of joy and success, but the real measure of a relationship is how we stand by each other during hardships.

Genuine friends offer their shoulders to lean on, providing unwavering support when it's needed the most. In this chapter, we shall explore the essence of relationships and how they contribute to our overall well-being.

Moreover, our usefulness to others peaks when we are present for them in times of their greatest need. It's about directing our resources and efforts to make a meaningful impact on others' lives. This doesn't necessarily require extraordinary measures; sometimes, the smallest acts of kindness can have the most profound effects. By being there for others, we not only uplift them, but we also find a deep sense of purpose and fulfillment in our own lives.

As I navigate through the highs and lows of life, I have come to appreciate the value of surrounding myself with supportive, empathetic, and positive individuals. These relationships foster success and well-being and contribute to our overall life satisfaction. Having a great relationship with others is not just about attracting exceptional people, but also about maintaining and nurturing those connections. By positioning ourselves in the right way, we naturally entice others who resonate with our values and aspirations.

In this chapter, I invite you to reflect on your networks and relationships. Are there people you've neglected in their times of need? How can you be more present and supportive of those who matter to you? Similarly, do you have people in your corner whom you can lean on during critical moments in your life? Exploring these questions can help us better understand the significance of our connections and how they shape our lives. Let's embark on this journey together, recognizing the power of networks and relationships in creating a fulfilling and meaningful life.

When It Matters the Most

We encounter people at various times and under different circumstances. We also extend ourselves to support those we care about. Numerous reasons and circumstances necessitate one person's presence in the life of another. For instance, you may attend a friend's birthday party, send a gift to someone you care about, visit a relative in the hospital, babysit a friend's children, contribute items to a local food bank or charity, or even offer your time as a volunteer. Acts of kindness are most beautiful when performed with genuine intentions and bring us a deep sense of fulfillment when we contribute positively to others' lives.

I have observed situations where showing up for someone profoundly touched their heart. Again, I'm reminded of my favorite saying: "A friend in need is a friend indeed." Giving me an extra orange when I already have ten might not deeply touch me, even though I'd appreciate it. Similarly, providing food to someone who isn't hungry or already has plenty may not have much impact. Two common mistakes people make are giving to those who already possess what they are receiving and giving with the expectation of reciprocation. While giving is great, it resonates more deeply when we give to those in dire need. Many individuals desperately need our support.

I conclude that the best time to show up for others is when they most require our assistance. This is when we make the most meaningful impact on their lives. By directing our resources and efforts rightly, we can accomplish much with whatever we have to create lasting impacts on others. Mike McIntyre, author of *The Kindness of Strangers: Penniless Across America*, remarked, "Sometimes those who give the most are the ones with the least to spare." We and our resources must be available when we are most needed.

Life consists of various stages: highs, lows, and everything in between. During our peak moments, many will gather around to share in our joys; naturally, people tend to join during good times. Success attracts many supporters who cherish celebratory times. Conversely, true friends are revealed during difficult times—when needs, lack, or trouble arises. Genuine friends stay with us, offering their shoulders to lean on, while those attracted only by abundance often fade away, turning their backs or becoming passive.

Where am I going with this? Reflect on your circle: are there people you've neglected in their time of need? Real friendship—or any connection—requires being present when it truly matters. Showing up only during happy, prosperous moments is insufficient. If you give a friend another pair of shoes when they already have five, it may be appreciated, but it is crucial to meet genuine needs. Don't abandon or distance yourself from those you've shared joyous times with should their situations change. Seek out those who need to be uplifted within your community and extend your hand when it matters most.

John Wesley wisely advised, "Employ whatever God has entrusted you with, in doing good, all possible good, in every possible kind and degree." *Those who do good attract others and possess an irresistible magnetism.* To be a person of value and significance, be someone who shows up for others when they need you the most.

Exploit Collective Capacity

I often view myself as an intelligent individual. However, no matter how smart I think I am, my knowledge and acumen are rather limited compared to the collective intelligence in the world. The same goes for you; you may be quick-witted, but your brilliance is just a small fraction of our collective genius. This should prompt us to reflect. Why would someone believe their idea surpasses those generated by a team of equally intelligent individuals? I have a secret to share: whenever I need to think of something significant at work, I gather my team to brainstorm together. The result is a treasure trove of ideas from brilliant minds, which we use to craft the best solution.

There is, however, a right way to do this. Many people in leadership positions assume their ideas are superior simply because of their authority. Managers often claim they seek input from their teams but then dictate specific plans, such as building a new office space with detailed specifications, and only ask for feedback. This approach stifles the team's creativity. If you already have a clear plan, communicate it rather than pretending to solicit input. But if you genuinely want innovative ideas, trust your team and engage them in brainstorming. Use their collective insights without assuming your idea is better.

Collaboration extends beyond generating ideas; it encompasses every aspect of human ability. Throughout my life, I've met many talented individuals who excel in various fields—arts, sciences, business—and showcase exceptional skills. However, even the most gifted person's contributions remain limited to their capabilities. While solo efforts might yield good results, achieving something truly remarkable requires teamwork. This is why a coordinated team effort was needed to conquer Mount Everest and why the moon landing involved numerous astronauts, scientists, engineers, program managers, and governmental support.

Many people struggle because they try to achieve greatness alone, forgetting that most monumental accomplishments result from collective effort. H.E. Luccock, a Methodist bishop, aptly said, "No one can whistle a symphony. It takes a whole orchestra to play it." Whenever I face a significant challenge, I consider who my teammates are, recognizing that other talented individuals can amplify my efforts. Stephen Covey, the author of *The 7 Habits of Highly Effective People,* emphasized, "Synergy is what happens when one plus one equals ten or a hundred or even a thousand! It's the profound result when two or more respectful human beings determine to go beyond their preconceived ideas to meet a great challenge."

The key is to stop struggling alone and figure out who else you can collaborate with to accomplish greater things. You may need to share the recognition, rewards, and outcomes with others, but isn't that the essence of life? Our goal is to create positive impacts, bring joy to others, achieve fulfillment, and contribute to a better world. In everything you do, always leverage the power of collective capacity for the greater good.

Surround Yourself With the Best People

Human beings are inherently social and crave relationships. If you question whether you need anyone at all, the answer may come in time. While it's possible to find contentment alone, sharing happiness with others enriches our lives. Interacting with others allows a mutual exchange of influence and growth.

We often fail to recognize the worth of those around us until they are no longer present. It's not only vital to attract exceptional individuals but also to maintain those connections. A synergistic brilliance tends to emerge when great minds congregate, and that's precisely the environment one aspires to be in: among intelligent and forward-thinking individuals.

Creating an ecosystem of supportive, empathetic, and positive people fosters success, well-being, and overall life satisfaction. However, forming meaningful relationships or connecting with quality people doesn't happen by chance. We attract individuals who mirror our own traits. To draw in friends, we must first exhibit friendliness ourselves. Enhancing ourselves to become the type of person others are drawn to is essential. A thriving relationship focuses on being the right person rather than merely finding the right person. Reflect on whether you are the right match for someone else before seeking out ideal companions.

Attracting remarkable people necessitates effort. Similar attracts similar—like begets like. It is often said that the outcomes you achieve are largely influenced by the five closest people to you. Consider your inner circle—do their life outcomes resonate with the future you envision for yourself?

It's crucial to make mindful decisions about whom we associate with, especially regarding self-improvement. Neale Donald Walsch, author of the *Conversations with God* series, aptly stated, "The purpose of a relationship is not to have another who might complete you, but to have another with whom you might share your completeness." By bettering ourselves, we naturally attract outstanding individuals. This is the key to surrounding oneself with the best people.

Let Them Help You Carry It

I have yet to meet anyone who requires absolutely no assistance from others. While some may give the impression of complete self-sufficiency, it is evident that this is not true. Throughout history and in contemporary times, even the most esteemed individuals have relied on the support of those around them. Those who choose to live in isolation miss out on the valuable support that could help them achieve their potential.

It can be argued that believing that one does not need help to accomplish significant tasks is a form of arrogance. Those bearing substantial responsibilities or possessing grand ideas must rely on others to make an impact that cannot be achieved alone.

Sometimes, what we carry isn't an innovative idea but a burden, a weight on our minds or lives that complicates things further. We often face challenges too heavy to shoulder alone. The truth is that humans are imperfect, and life inevitably presents difficulties. None of us is exempt from life's burdens and issues. Nevertheless, we do not have to struggle alone. During times of heavy burdens, seeking help from others is both needed and wise.

What are you carrying? Are your responsibilities at home, work, or in your community overwhelming? Do you have a task so large you recognize you cannot tackle it by yourself? Perhaps you are dealing with substantial challenges. This message emphasizes the importance of allowing others to assist you. When the load becomes too heavy, accept the help offered by those willing to lend a hand.

"Accepting help doesn't make you weak. It's like catching your breath so you can stand up again and help others. When one person is down, the other one is up," said Morgan L. Busse, author of the *Following the Word* series. We should abandon the notion of being superheroes. Everyone needs help. If someone offers genuine assistance, accept it gratefully and let them help you bear the load.

Let Someone Else Drive the Car

Achievers often arrive at their dreamland, which might be a state of fulfillment, an impressive level of success, or the zenith of their career. People attain these higher achievements at various stages in life, with some reaching their goals earlier and others later. Regardless of the timing, finally attaining the most rewarding phase of one's efforts is always gratifying, so gratifying in fact that one can become overconfident and do whatever it takes to prolong it.

How do I know this? When individuals start to achieve considerable success, garner immense respect, or receive accolades and praise, they usually wish for it to continue indefinitely. This desire can lead to people becoming selfish, arrogant, and insensitive. Particularly when they wield power, they have a strong inclination to cling to it tightly.

Consider why politicians relentlessly pursue reelection or why corporate executives resist stepping down. What causes people's reluctance to pass the baton and insistence on remaining in control? We must recognize that nothing lasts forever. Everything, whether a prosperous period or a challenging one, is ephemeral. When we find ourselves in significant positions, we should prepare others to carry forward our work. Many legacies and accomplishments fade into obscurity because people held on too long, missing the opportunity to pass the baton due to selfishness and greed.

The key point here is this: you don't need to cling to your current role, opportunity, or authority indefinitely. Life can be likened to a board game where each player occupies spaces left by another. Some will create space, while others will fill it. If you have the chance to create new opportunities, do so, and allow others to step into the roles you leave behind. That reminds me of an old saying, "Seize the day, then let it go," by, I believe, Marty Rubin, author of *The Boiled Frog Syndrome*. You can blaze a trail, enabling others to follow. But remember, most people can only drive so far. You don't have to keep going until you deplete your ideas and energy or become irrelevant. Let someone else take the wheel and build on the legacy you leave.

As crucial as it is to leverage relationships and networks to reach the pinnacle of your endeavors, it's equally important to uplift others and let them step into the roles you will vacate. We must understand that the purpose of self-improvement, gaining others' goodwill, and mastering personal charisma isn't for self-aggrandizement but to advance society's greater good. Giving others a chance to shine is integral to this mission.

Be the Advocate Not the Judge

Do you believe you possess the moral authority to adjudicate others' situations? Likely not. Yet this is what many of us try to do daily. We often rush to conclude who people are, their intentions, motives, and dispositions. We evaluate them based on our personal criteria and then assess their abilities, skills, and potential according to our standards, shaping our opinion of who they are. This approach has pervaded our interactions with others; we draw conclusions too hastily. We assume the role of judge over others' characters despite not measuring up to those very standards ourselves. Such hypocrisy!

Our true responsibility, however, is to act as advocates: individuals who support, defend, and champion others' interests. Each of us has someone we can speak up for. Often, what people need from us isn't particularly strenuous. In most cases, we merely need to bolster or amplify those voices who might otherwise go unheard. Our goal should be to stand in the gap for those around us and become a voice for the voiceless.

Consider your influence in your workplace, home, or community. You'll notice numerous disadvantaged individuals. They may miss out on jobs, team selections, contracts, promotions, or aid or fail to realize their potential unless you advocate for them. If everyone is a judge, who will champion another's cause? We need more advocates than judges. Envision a world where we all support each other, advocating for one another's causes.

I urge you to become an advocate. Some people need your support, guidance, advocacy, and action for their benefit. Fulfillment in life comes not from judging others but from the positive impact we make on their lives. The reason some remain unhappy and unfulfilled is that they've taken on the wrong role—that of a judge instead of an advocate. "Nothing exalts the soul or gives it a sheer sense of buoyancy and victory so much as being used to change the lives of other people," said E. Stanley Jones, a Methodist theologian. Let us abandon our roles as judges and embrace our new responsibilities as advocates for others. I challenge you to find a hand to hold and inspire hope in others.

Find A Hand to Hold and Inspire Hope

Nobody possesses anything in this world that hasn't been given to them. Reflect on your journey from your earliest memories to the present moment. Could you have come this far without assistance of any kind? Although some people have had far less help and faced greater challenges—this is understood—any breakthrough we achieve still involves the support and generosity of others.

It's true that no one achieves success and great accomplishments effortlessly. However, the stories behind the successes and achievements of most remarkable individuals often highlight the role of connections, collaboration, and the involvement of others. You've likely benefited from advice, recommendations, mentorship, sponsorship, support, or kindness from someone. Achieving great feats or reaching significant heights aren't possible by being entirely self-reliant. The leverage we gain from others supporting us is substantial.

However, this message isn't about us merely enjoying benefits from others; it's about becoming a source of support for others. It's about assisting others in reaching their goals. We must not underestimate the importance of the sponsorship, support, or recommendations we provide to those who are earnest about their futures. You and I may hold the key that opens doors to blessings and breakthroughs for those around us. Sometimes all someone needs to succeed is an introduction, a recommendation, or a bit of guidance. While these tasks may seem simple, they demand genuine and deliberate effort on our part. The question is whether we accept this responsibility or not.

Rather than only helping others when it's convenient for us, could we try to find someone to uplift? Can we assist someone in achieving something they currently cannot do alone? Can you offer something freely to someone who cannot repay you and expect nothing in return?

What is critical but difficult for someone else might be simple for you, though it might cost you a bit too. Regardless, there is immense joy and fulfillment that comes from offering help to others without expecting anything in return. Remember the words of E. Stanley Jones from the last section: "Nothing exalts the soul or gives it a sheer sense of buoyancy and victory so much as being used to change the lives of other people."

More importantly, the help we provide becomes a wellspring of hope and inspiration. By supporting someone in achieving something significant, we signify that their efforts can lead to success, helping build their confidence for even greater things ahead.

Supporting others, however, doesn't mean providing handouts without accountability. It means rallying around someone who is making a committed effort to achieve their goals and has a strong determination to succeed. After all, everyone is ultimately responsible for their own outcomes.

Here's a call to carry someone else and participate in their journey toward significant achievements. If you look around, you will find many individuals who need what you can offer. Perhaps you've achieved a place of honor, repute, and grace. That means you can bless others. Some may say, "But I also need help. I am not there yet." They're correct; even those who can help others need help themselves. This is why we must spread help and support one another. Who will you uplift today? Find a hand to hold and inspire hope in others.

Hold Them in High Esteem

One essential principle I uphold is to respect, admire, value, and praise those who work alongside me. Have you ever experienced a moment when someone acknowledged your efforts, whether significant or minor? How did it make you feel? Did it motivate you to repeat the action, perhaps even better than before?

Recognition fosters encouragement. When people receive acknowledgment, they are inspired to do more. Valuing and honoring individuals for their contributions instills a sense of achievement and reinforces their self-belief. It elevates their morale.

Failing to appreciate someone's accomplishment, contribution, or milestone can be akin to belittling them. Be mindful! If your employees, team members, children, or those you lead achieve something and you downplay their efforts, you risk losing their respect. People typically respond positively to affirmations, accolades, awards, praise, and thank-you notes. The individuals you value are more likely to remain loyal to you.

Those you respect will, in turn, respect you, as respect begets respect.

We must give honor where it is due. Consider those who work for or with you. Reflect on how enriching our workplaces, families, communities, and society would be if we all valued, respected, and honored one another. The Swiss philosopher Henri Frederic Amiel once said, "There is no respect for others without humility in oneself." This rings true; we can all practice humility to foster respect for others.

Imagine a world where people are appreciated for who they are, the good they have accomplished, and what they can achieve. Envision a workplace, team, family, or organization where everyone genuinely acknowledges others' contributions. It is time to hold those around us in high esteem, recognizing them for their actions and potential benefits to society. Remember, this is not solely about you but about the greater good of society.

CHAPTER 4 SUMMARY

In this chapter, we explored the profound impact of networks and relationships on our lives. The key lessons highlight the importance of genuine connections, the power of showing up for others, and the value of surrounding ourselves with supportive individuals. By reflecting on our relationships, we can better understand how they shape our experiences and contribute to our overall well-being. Here are some quick highlights:

1. The importance of networks and relationships
    - The people we surround ourselves with significantly influence our experiences and successes. Genuine connections are tested during difficult times, and true friends offer unwavering support when needed most.

2. The power of showing up
   - Being present for others, especially during their challenging times, creates a ripple effect of positivity and fulfillment. Small acts of kindness, performed with genuine intentions, can have profound impacts.
3. The value of supportive individuals
   - Surrounding oneself with supportive, empathetic, and positive individuals fosters success, well-being, and overall life satisfaction. It's essential to maintain and nurture these connections by being the person who naturally attracts others with similar values.
4. Reflecting on relationships
   - It's crucial to reflect on our networks and relationships, ensuring we are present and supportive for those who matter to us. By doing so, we can better understand the significance of our connections and how they shape our lives.

CHAPTER 4 REFLECTIONS FOR ACTION

It's time to act on what you have learned in this chapter. Kindly read the reflection questions in the following table, and in the space provided, note what actions you will take and when.

	Reflection Questions
1	Reflect on whether you have distanced yourself from someone who genuinely needs your support. Resolve to be consistently present for those with whom you've shared memorable moments, regardless of their current circumstances. Offer yourself as a reliable source of comfort and assistance.
	Notes to self:

2	Do you lead or work in a team? How effectively do you use your team's collective intelligence to generate ideas? Consider a goal you're struggling with. Are you out of ideas? Can you seek advice from someone or a team?
	Notes to self:
3	Is there a project or task that you realize requires collaboration to achieve excellence? If so, seek out individuals who can join you in this endeavor. Similarly, consider how you can support someone else striving to achieve something remarkable. Find an opportunity to assist and offer your help.
	Notes to self:
4	It's important to evaluate your relationships. What types of individuals do you draw into your life? Reflect on those nearest to you. Consider if these are truly the people you wish to be connected with.
	Notes to self:
5	Reflect on your own situation. Are you in need of assistance? If help is being offered, accept it or reach out to someone who can genuinely support you. In turn, you can also be a source of

	aid for others. Identify someone in need and offer your help willingly and unconditionally. *Notes to self:*
6	Consider your present role, authority, or achievements. Is there an individual you can mentor to assume your responsibilities as you progress to new opportunities? Recognizing the impermanence of life, it's wise to formulate a strategy for when you no longer hold the influence, power, or vigor you currently do. *Notes to self:*
7	Conduct a self-assessment. Have you acted more as a judge than an advocate? If so, consider reversing course by shifting your focus from judgment to advocacy. What concrete steps can you take to support and stand up for others? Identify a specific individual in need of your advocacy. Document the actions you plan to take and ensure you follow through. *Notes to self:*
8	Reflect on two or three colleagues you've worked with recently and send them a note appreciating their efforts. Express your respect for their contributions humbly. Make it a habit to

acknowledge those who work with or for you. Forgive anyone who belittled you and show better character by valuing and respecting others.

Notes to self:

CHAPTER 5

EMBRACE SUCCESS IN ALL FACETS OF LIFE

Every job is a self-portrait of the person who did it. Autograph your work with excellence.

~ Ted Key ~

What did you think when you saw the title of this chapter? You may wonder about the connection between embracing success and mastering personal magnetism. Well, people generally associate with successful people. One way to draw people to us is by becoming successful in what we do. It is not surprising that successful people have many associations.

Success is one of the most sought-after and celebrated concepts in our society. There have been several thousands—or more—of books written on success. In fact, our society is obsessed with success such that an average person spends their entire life trying to become successful. We often admire and praise those who have achieved success in their fields, and we aspire to emulate their accomplishments.

Success is often challenging to achieve due to society's narrow view of what it means to succeed. People widely believe that success is synonymous with wealth and popularity, and that affects the general mindset. It appears society suggests if we don't conform to a particular standard, we lack value. This perception of success contributes to widespread feelings of low self-worth.

Yet isn't it possible that success could be defined in various ways across various aspects of life, including career, personal relationships, health, and overall well-being?

Another false narrative prevalent in society is depicting success as being synonymous with happiness for those who align with socially accepted norms. It is assumed that having more material things and being famous mean becoming happy.

Others give the impression that significant achievements come easily, without acknowledging the typical hindrances one might face on their journey to success. Challenges such as fear, doubt, rejection, criticism, and stress are often overlooked. Consequently, many individuals find themselves ill-equipped to tackle these obstacles and fail to cultivate resilience, courage, self-assurance, and the necessary skills to cope.

Understanding the key factors behind success and adopting the habits of prosperous individuals, such as establishing purpose, defining objectives, organizing, setting priorities, acquiring knowledge, building connections, and cooperating, set us on a trajectory toward reaping significant benefits. It is gratifying to experience and acknowledge the favorable results that come with success, including contentment, a sense of achievement, acknowledgment, and influence.

What truly constitutes success? What approaches can we adopt in our thinking and daily habits to encourage success in every facet of our existence? What is the importance of attaining success, and how does it relate to enhancing personal charm? How might we harness our inherent talents, enthusiasms, and magnetism to generate prospects and build relationships that contribute to our triumph?

The purpose of this chapter is to inspire, encourage, and embolden you to chase your ambitions and to remind you to savor both the journey and the outcomes of your dedication. My goal is to help you recognize that there is a vast array of ways in which success can manifest and to hold in high esteem the diverse choices and journeys others may take on their quests for fulfillment. Through this chapter, you will attain a more profound appreciation for the nature of success and the multiple manners it can manifest in.

Ultimately, you will learn how to leverage your life's successes to cultivate positive relationships and achieve esteemed personal stature and respect from your peers throughout your endeavors. Let us begin the journey.

Success Has Many Friends

Success is a concept that varies widely from person to person. What may represent the pinnacle of achievement, such as reaching the peak of Mount Everest, for one person could be as simple as acquiring a new pair of shoes for another. Whether it's buying a house, graduating from college, getting married, writing a book, making music, winning a Nobel Prize, learning to walk, or yearning to reach the stars, success is shaped by an individual's circumstances, background, life phase, necessities, goals, determination, and mindset.

Understanding that success is not universally defined can assist us in tempering our expectations of ourselves and others. We often measure another's performance based on our personal benchmarks and expectations, acting as judges of their success without a mutual understanding of what constitutes achievement. With no common standard to align with, success remains a subjective and personal matter. Nonetheless, striving for success in all our endeavors is commendable.

Moreover, it is generally known that success has many friends. Success tends to attract companionship. Being successful typically draws people to you as success acts as a powerful social magnet. People usually favor the company of those who are thriving. The opposite is true for failure or poverty. Achieving success means gaining recognition and forming associations; people want to claim connection with someone who has accomplished something worthwhile.

Ultimately, being successful can enhance one's charisma and draw others to us. We should each define success for ourselves, cultivate it, and anticipate its fruition. However, in our definition of success, we must consider our potential, our gifts and abilities, and the opportunities available to us, and center our supreme goal on our life's purpose. I dealt with the subject of purpose extensively in my book, *Pursuit of Personal Leadership*. Perhaps you might find it helpful.

By setting and fulfilling our own goals, we unlock the potential for opportunity and social affiliations. Success contributes to shaping your ability to attract others, an element of honing your personal allure.

What You Need to Get Everything Else

You may be familiar with the phrase, "You don't know what you don't know." Equal opportunities do not necessarily mean equal outcomes. Even if two individuals are given the same chances, their paths can diverge drastically over time. Moreover, a head start in life is advantageous, but it doesn't ensure that someone will finish ahead.

In observing those who excel, I've noticed a constant attribute regardless of their education, background, prior opportunities, or current success status. The fact is, those who manage to progress in life typically possess knowledge and take actions that are uncommon among the average population. As straightforward as it may appear, one crucial factor for success is knowing what you need at the right time. Many people suffer from ignorance, which is certainly not an asset.

Now I'll share a discovery that's been pivotal in my life. Perhaps it may help change your approach and enable you to control your own success trajectory. Achieving success isn't as intimidating or insurmountable as you might assume. You just need to learn and do a bit more than the average individual in your field. This concept of rising above the norm and having that extra something aligns well with Spanish philosopher, Baltasar Gracian's, words, "Knowledge and courage are the elements of greatness." We must aspire to gain better knowledge and find the bravery to act on it.

As I mentioned in my book, *Pursuit of Personal Leadership,* you don't require Albert Einstein's brilliance or Beethoven's artistry to advance in life. A marginal increase above what is common, above the average, often suffices. Starting with superior information followed by added effort sets you apart and transforms the ordinary into the extraordinary.

I have witnessed seemingly unremarkable individuals lead and succeed in significant endeavors. It's about differentiating oneself to achieve distinction. Remember, success attracts followers. Adding that "extra" to the ordinary secures your place among distinguished company and is key to mastering personal appeal.

There's No Perfect Way to Succeed

Observing individuals fixated on a particular thing they must do or become in life or a certain ambition, I find myself reflecting on whether they've truly acknowledged the vast array of opportunities available in the world. The notion of an ideal path to success is misleading as there is no one-size-fits-all career or pursuit reserved for creating affluence, prosperity, or power.

Consider the metaphor of a mountain and the numerous ways it can be navigated: it can be climbed over, tunneled through, excavated beneath, or even dismantled entirely. We must all be open to alternate routes and multiple options. Being closed-minded can lead us to overlook potentially greater alternatives.

Maintaining a narrow or limited perspective is a luxury we cannot afford. For example, life offers a plethora of career options, from doctor to teacher, nurse to soldier, engineer to truck driver, etc. Your life's direction is primarily a matter of choice, and keeping your options wide open is advisable at the outset.

Reflect on your current phase in life, whether in work, business, or any other venture. There's no singular perfect tactic for success. Let your thoughts wander to other approaches. Encourage innovative thinking rather than conforming to established methods or perceived sole solutions. Embrace adaptability.

Open-mindedness has led numerous people to discover their true callings. "An open-minded person sees life without boundaries, whereas a close-minded person can only see what's beyond their eyes," said Kaoru Shinmon, author of *My Journey Stepping into Sunshine*. By opening ourselves up to what could be, we position ourselves to make choices backed by clear insight. This approach should not be confused with a lack of direction; it simply means we're not afraid to reevaluate our actions to improve upon them.

Success is more about the voyage than reaching the destination, and there is certainly no flawless method to achieving it. It's the willingness to recognize and address relevant societal issues that mark our progress. In uncovering and tackling these issues, we not only increase our own visibility but also inspire and elevate others as we move toward our collective success.

The End Is Better, so Get to the End

As each of the past years ended, I found myself reflecting on the year, contemplating how effectively I utilized it. Despite starting the year with detailed planning, it became clear to me that the execution and completion near the year's end held more weight. The start of the year brought with it just a plan and the determination to achieve great accomplishments, yet it was the fruition of those plans and the finished work that truly marked the value of the year for me. I took great satisfaction in the plentiful outcomes of my efforts.

Indeed, the conclusion of an endeavor generally holds more significance than its commencement. Recognition and rewards typically follow the completion of a task. In any race, attaining a medal is contingent on finishing, not merely running swiftly. Thus, irrespective of your speed, even if you outpace one of the fastest animals like a cheetah, without completion, there can be no reward. You will not have crossed the finish line, where rewards are customarily bestowed.

This leads to my next point: Throughout life, we often embark on pursuits only to abandon them at the first sign of difficulty. We set forth on paths and give up when the journey proves arduous. At times, dreams and strategies are forsaken upon encountering seemingly insurmountable challenges. This means we fall short, forfeiting any potential rewards.

As we navigate life, we must kindle within ourselves the tenacity to both initiate and conclude whatever we aspire to achieve. There are no accolades for retraction. Only by seeing through our endeavors can we attain fulfillment. To draw from the book of Ecclesiastes 7:8, "Finishing is better than starting. Patience is better than pride." The world awaits your contributions, eager for the expression of your best qualities.

It begins with formulating a viable strategy for success and ensuring that actions align with plans. *Ambition accompanied by diligence leads to accomplishments.* Conversely, giving up or abandoning the journey will never lead us to our desired destination. Do not halt your stride. Continue to strive forward. Persist in your undertakings. Your gratification lies ahead.

My wish for you is that you have the boldness to dream big and bring your dreams to fruition across all facets of life. By doing so, you'll observe the world gravitating to you, eager to partake in the rich results of your labors—a testament to your command of personal allure.

Stop for a Moment and Fix It

Have you ever attempted to ride a bicycle with flat tires? How smoothly did it go? And have you ever tried using a dull knife in the kitchen or a dull ax to cut wood? We often take for granted the ease of driving a functional car, but when it breaks down, it ceases to be of use. I've even had the frustrating experience of struggling with a defective can opener. It was hardly worth the effort. When items are damaged or not maintained well, they fail to perform effectively, or at all.

So why do we persistently use malfunctioning items and expect them to work perfectly? And beyond that, why do we continually harbor damage in our lives and hope for excellent results?

If your bonds with important people are fractured, mend them. If you're emotionally hurt, seek healing. If your career path is shattered, take steps to rebuild it. If any aspect of your life seems in disrepair, pause to fix it. Continuing to function with anything impaired is simply a sinkhole. You cannot succeed if you are not whole.

Often, mending what's broken involves researching solutions, collaborating with others, or seeking assistance. Don't hesitate to ask for help if you need it. The goal is always restoration because things operating at their best ensure efficiency. Take familial relationships, for instance. A healthy family relationship enables joint achievements, whereas a strained one stifles progress. Professor and video game designer Jesse Schell said, "Usually, the best ideas come from having to fix a really hard problem."

This is a call for restoration and correction, putting everything back in order or repairing what is damaged to regain completeness. Take the time to address and solve issues; mend anything that's not working well. By doing so, you will maximize your ability to succeed.

Sometimes, the focus isn't just on repair but also on buttressing something valuable, particularly in terms of our relationships. It's crucial to be deliberate in how we interact with those around us. Those who invest in building strong bonds and fostering significant connections end up with a supportive circle of friends. The caliber of individuals in our lives shapes our experiences, which in turn influences our thoughts and actions.

Classy Is Not Cocky, so Be Stylish

People widely acknowledged and admired in their professions demonstrate remarkable skill and dedication. This isn't coincidental. Consider a handful of accomplished individuals you know, and it becomes apparent they approach their work distinctively from others. They introduce a unique quality that sets them apart. They consistently strive to reach the pinnacle of excellence in their field.

Investing average effort typically yields average outcomes. Moreover, our work garners recognition when executed with finesse and optimal proficiency. Many remain indistinguishable because their work fails to stand out; it lacks distinction.

Sophistication should not be mistaken for arrogance. To embody sophistication means infusing your work with refinement and exceptional attentiveness. You don't have to be the most skilled, but you should be the most meticulous. By incorporating precision and consideration into everything you do, you'll be noticed among the masses. It's all about excelling as an individual and elevating the caliber of your work to its zenith.

If your role is in sales, approach it with inventiveness like Da Vinci. If you teach, do so with the vigor of Mike Tyson. If painting is your craft, approach it with a creativity akin to Mozart. Always aim to go over and above mediocrity in your endeavors. Foster excellence and a distinctive flair in everything you undertake. Continually question how you can innovate to yield something truly outstanding.

Consider luxury car brands such as Mercedes or Lexus. Beyond their material quality, buying these vehicles is an investment in the prestige the brands carry. Driving a Porsche or a Ferrari is synonymous with elegance. Hence, this is an invitation for you to exemplify yourself and your work; be the Mercedes or Ferrari within your sphere. I once saw a quote by Ted Key, cartoonist and creator of such shows as *Mr. Peabody & Sherman*, who said, "Every job is a self-portrait of the person who did it. Autograph your work with excellence." When you align class with stellar performance and excel at your craft, you'll attract those who value your excellence. Embrace elegance in your professional and personal pursuits and you will see the world line up to partake in the brilliant outcome of your endeavor.

Don't Arrive Without Experiencing the Journey

I've driven along Canada's Highway 401 on numerous occasions. I often drive around the speed limit, yet it intrigues me that approximately half the vehicles on the highway overtake me. This leads me to question their destination and the urgency behind their acceleration. It appears to be a human inclination to want to reach places swiftly.

The desire for haste seems to permeate various facets of our lives. Why are we often in pursuit of rapid progress, whether in education, wealth, relationships, career advancement, or success? We might concentrate so intently on our objectives and the result that we wish to achieve them sooner rather than later.

One major downside to this rush is overlooking the journey itself. Our preoccupation with the endpoint means missing out on the travel experience itself. For instance, driving too fast on the highway may cause you to overlook the scenic views as you pass the landscapes, cityscapes, other vehicles, and even warnings that could save you from speeding tickets or collisions.

Life should be about savoring each moment, not just rushing through it. Enjoy your job, cherish time with family, relish the years spent with your children or grandchildren, embrace your college days, and appreciate every part of life. Experiences are meant to be shared, and those who accompany us on our paths are important. It's crucial to value these relationships rather than fixating solely on our goals.

Ultimately, many people realize at life's conclusion that it wasn't the achievements but the experiences gathered while pursuing them that mattered most. The person you develop into and the experiences you undergo along your path to success far outweigh the success itself. "Life is a daring adventure toward an unknown future. Its beauty depends on how much you enjoy the journey," remarked Debasish Mridha, a physician, philosopher, and author. Life isn't just about attaining goals; it's about the richness of the journey. Ensure you don't reach the end without having truly lived the voyage.

Celebrate Your Wins and Be Grateful

"I wept for not having shoes until I met a man without legs." That phrase stuck with me, though I can't recall where I first heard it. Many attribute it to Helen Keller, though Persian poet, Saadi Shirazi, wrote that sentiment centuries earlier. Either way, that one sentence tells us it's too easy to fixate on what we lack or wish to attain and fail to appreciate our current possessions.

Cultivating gratitude is a deliberate practice. In the same way we dedicate time, space, and resources to achieving great feats, we should also focus on acknowledging our successes and being thankful for what we have. We ought to let joy fill our hearts and let ourselves be exhilarated by positive thoughts.

Do you take time to recognize your personal accomplishments? Often, we may become preoccupied with unfinished goals. As a college student, one might overlook the enjoyment of completing each academic year while awaiting graduation. When constructing a house, one might forget to celebrate completing the foundation or roofing in their eagerness to move in.

There are compelling reasons to embrace gratitude. A joyful heart harbors hope for what's ahead. Individuals who remain thankful, regardless of their situations, possess an admirable life stance. They understand life's inherent value and avoid losing the very essence that propels them forward. Joy mirrors the tranquility within us and fortifies us to continue our pursuits. Model Alek Wek once said, "The most beautiful things are not associated with money; they are memories and moments. If you don't celebrate those, they can pass you by."

Seize every opportunity to celebrate, not just the monumental victories. Establish great ambitions yet divide them into manageable segments that can be frequently acknowledged. This approach gives a sense of progress, fueling further achievements.

Consider why we receive paychecks regularly instead of after many years or many accomplishments. Earnings recognized weekly or monthly signify meaningful contributions deserving of compensation. Similarly, shouldn't you reward yourself for minor achievements as you look forward to greater ones?

As you journey through life, reflect on your present status and find reasons for gratitude. Allocate time to honor your victories each year. Recognize your experiences and express thanks for them all—including both pleasant and challenging times. Despite the hardships and setbacks, remember they are transient. Life's spectrum encompasses both troughs and peaks.

Ponder your future and derive vigor from the present. Celebrate and maintain positivity, which will attract favorable individuals to your side. Recall *The Fact of Life's* Charlotte Rae's words: "I want to tell everybody to celebrate every day, to savor the day and be good to yourself, love yourself, and then you can be good to others and be of service to others." Your contentment, happiness, and the jubilant environment you sustain will offer others a refuge for comfort. Your positive life will draw other people close to you, making you a center of attraction.

CHAPTER 5 SUMMARY

This chapter offered insights and lessons on how to define, pursue, and enjoy success, with the aim to inspire and encourage you to chase your personal ambitions, savor the journey, and cultivate positive relationships. Here are the key lessons:

1. Success is a personal and subjective concept that varies from person to person. Yet successful people attract companionship. People are generally drawn to those who have achieved accomplishments.
2. Success requires knowing what you need at the right time and doing a bit more than the average person in your field. It is about going above and beyond mediocrity.
3. Success is not limited to one perfect way or path, but rather it involves being open-minded and adaptable to different opportunities and approaches.
4. Success is more about the journey than the destination, and it is important to enjoy and appreciate each moment and experience along the way. It is especially important to enjoy life's journey with those around us.
5. Success is enhanced by a touch of excellence and elegance in your work, which sets you apart from the masses and attracts recognition. People notice those who are outstanding.
6. Success is also a matter of restoration and correction, which means fixing what is broken and seeking help when needed.
7. Success should be celebrated and acknowledged, not just for the big achievements but also for the small ones, and gratitude should be cultivated for what you have. Content and happy people are attractive, which draws others close to them.

CHAPTER 5 REFLECTIONS FOR ACTION

It's time to act on what you have learned in this chapter. Kindly read the reflection questions in the following table, and in the space provided, note what actions you will take and when.

	Reflection Questions
1	Reflecting on your career and professional ambitions, articulate what success signifies for you in two sentences. What actions can you undertake this week to bring yourself closer to achieving your definition of success?
	Notes to self:
2	Assess your current expertise level. Do you possess a higher-than-average understanding of your field? Strive to expand your knowledge base. Pursue further education and challenge yourself to exceed mediocrity by dedicating additional time and effort to your activities. The outcomes will be impressive.
	Notes to self:
3	When was the last time you evaluated your approach to your current tasks or projects? Reflect on an ongoing project or work responsibility. Could there be a more efficient method? If you could turn back the clock by five years, what single change would you make? What steps can you take now to address it?
	Notes to self:

4	Reflect on your current circumstances. Is everything functioning smoothly? If not, what are the reasons? Identify areas for improvement that could save you time and enhance the efficiency of your life and then take action to address them.
	Notes to self:
5	Consider a product or service you offer. Are you confident it is of the highest quality? Regardless of what you are currently working on, take a moment to slow down and reflect. What steps can you take to enhance it further? Strive to maintain a high level of professionalism and always infuse your work with a touch of excellence.
	Notes to self:
6	It's important to take a moment and assess your progress. Are you finding joy in the path you're on? Is it necessary to decelerate to fully embrace your journey's highlights? The choice is yours. Make a conscious effort to notice the small details that appear each day. Allow yourself the opportunity to appreciate and savor your experiences as you strive for success.
	Notes to self:

7	Identify and list five distinct aspects of your life for which you feel gratitude. Reflect on these aspects briefly, then make plans to celebrate. Did you overlook an opportunity to celebrate something recently? Is it still possible for you to celebrate it now? Document specific things that you will always choose to celebrate in the future. Set a reminder to help you remember these occasions. Maintain an attitude of gratitude.
	Notes to self:

CHAPTER 6

LET YOUR CREATIVITY AND INNOVATION SPEAK

I've found that luck is quite predictable. If you want more luck, take more chances. Be more active. Show up more often.

~ Brian Tracy ~

I am regularly reminded of the profound impact of creativity and innovation on our lives. One way to make the world take us seriously is through our creativity and innovation. Creativity is not merely a luxury reserved for artists and inventors; it is the lifeblood of progress and problem-solving in our everyday existence. Innovation propels us forward, challenging the status quo and opening doors to new possibilities. Together, creativity and innovation are powerful enough to transform our dreams into reality.

Creativity and the drive for innovation have led to breakthroughs that seemed impossible at first. My journey as an author of many books is an example. Little did I know that by embracing my writing ability, I could bring transformative messages to a world that desperately needs them. I've learned that the key to unlocking our creative potential lies in our willingness to embrace new horizons, to step out of our comfort zones, and to persist despite the uncertainties that lie ahead. We must develop the courage to pursue our grandest ambitions.

In this chapter, I invite you to explore what it means to let your creativity and innovation speak. We will journey through the significance of nurturing a fertile mind, one that transcends trivial conversations and engages with ideas that can change the world. I will discuss how to be relevant in a rapidly changing world by continually seeking new horizons and focusing on key issues that drive meaningful outcomes. Those who are creative and innovative become forces to reckon with.

We will examine the transformative power of light—in other words, knowledge—that dispels the darkness of ignorance and guides us toward enlightened thinking. This chapter will challenge you to evaluate your current state, identify the factors holding you back, and create actionable plans to overcome barriers. By doing so, you set the stage for personal growth, achieving your long-held dreams, and developing an attractive personality irresistible to others.

As we embark on this journey together, think of this chapter as a catalyst for your own creative and innovative pursuits. Let it inspire you to harness your potential and manifest the extraordinary ideas that reside within you. Welcome to a world where your imagination knows no bounds and your innovative spirit leads the way. Let us step forward with confidence and curiosity, ready to transform our visions into reality, thereby building a personality that cannot be ignored.

Find New Horizons

I've noticed something intriguing: many individuals have aspirations they haven't pursued, destinations they haven't visited, and dreams they've yet to realize. When people share their true desires with me, I ask them why they haven't begun taking steps to achieve them. My real question is, "What is holding you back?"

We deprive ourselves of life's best experiences when we intend to achieve great things but lack the courage to take the first step. Often, we're dissatisfied with our current situation but continue to cling to what prevents us from progressing. What is holding you back?

I have seen people ask those in midlife, "If you could advise your eighteen-year-old self, what would your advice be?" However, reflecting on past hypothetical advice doesn't seem productive as the past is unchangeable. Instead, imagine you are ninety. How would you reflect on your life? Would you celebrate achieving your dreams or lament opportunities missed due to hesitation?

I ask, "What is holding you back?" Many of us are restrained by jobs, activities, and relationships that influence our long-term decisions based on short-term experiences. We allow present comfort and temporary satisfaction to hinder our long-term achievements, settling for "good" instead of pursuing what is "right." This results in stagnation rather than progress because we avoid disturbances in our routine, leading to a complacent and unfulfilled life.

However, life shouldn't be monotonous, tedious, or repetitive. William Faulkner said, "You cannot swim for new horizons until you have the courage to lose sight of the shore." Progress is attained by constant forward movement. No matter who you are or what you have done in the past, this is not your destination; you must seek new horizons. If you've recently achieved significant goals and feel content, it's time to dream bigger. Complacency is not a virtue; success is an ongoing journey, not a final stop.

Life's journey is like a rollercoaster, with peaks and valleys, continuous cycles of completion, and new beginnings. *Life is a perpetual adventure, prompting us to constantly seek new perspectives, forge ahead, and muster the courage to keep moving.*

Again, I ask, "What is holding you back?" Do you need a new niche, job, association, or opportunity? Do you need to acquire new skills, switch industries, or start a new business? Whatever your situation, look forward, find new horizons, and act.

Discovering new horizons maintains your relevance in the world. No one wants to board a train that has reached its destination. Having new goals and adventures is key to personal growth and allure. When your journey aligns with others' ambitions, they will join you and contribute to your path. Avoid stagnation; keep that train moving.

Develop a Strong and Insightful Mind

Avoid engaging in trivial conversations. The topics discussed by great minds differ significantly from those preferred by individuals with average or narrow perspectives. Mediocre individuals often consider themselves moderate, but they merely exhibit their limited, low-quality, and ignorant viewpoint on everything.

I recall a conversation from several years ago with a group of individuals, wherein someone remarked, "You guys just talk in millions of dollars." That's accurate. I am comfortable managing affairs worth millions of dollars, and I speak in such terms when appropriate. In fact, I look forward to the day when my discussions will be routinely focused on billions of dollars.

Note that my point isn't about the amount of money; it's about the mindset. Mediocre thinkers do not perceive or converse in the same manner as great minds. Great minds, because of their worldview, discuss ideas: large concepts that surpass the understanding of those with mediocre minds. On the other hand, those with narrower perspectives focus on material things without appreciating how those things came into existence. The key difference is that a great mind operates on the level of ideas, while an average mind functions at the level of material possessions.

All the magnificent creations we see in our world today started as ideas conceived by great minds. To achieve greatness, you must become a visionary and cultivate your ideas. Mastery of any significant endeavor in the world comes through implementing ideas. Without your own ideas, you end up serving those who do have them. Individuals who possess ideas govern the world, whereas those lacking ideas are governed.

This is a call to liberate yourself from narrow-mindedness and mediocrity. Abstain from negligible conversations and align yourself with those who think profoundly. Expand your thinking and observe how your language evolves. When your mind overflows with ideas and you clearly understand your ambitions, you will transition from being among the governed to becoming one who governs.

Washington Irving, author of "The Legend of Sleepy Hollow," once said, "Little minds are tamed and subdued by misfortune; but great minds rise above them." Utilizing your imagination and acting on your ideas shape not only your life but also the lives of others. Developing a strong and insightful mind attracts numerous people eager to join your journey. This is one key to mastering personal magnetism.

Let It Spring to Life

Spring is undoubtedly my favorite season. Following winter, which is notably cold and severe here in Canada, spring offers a much-needed respite and heralds the beginning of the planting season.

During spring, every time I gaze through my windows, I observe the grass turning green, signaling the anticipation of newborn blooms and the revitalization of trees and bushes. Despite the allure of spring, I do not typically engage in planting, although I have done so in the past. However, I watch my neighbors and friends tending to their planting, sowing seeds into the fertile soil and anticipating new life. It is uplifting to see plants germinate and grow, showcasing the marvelous workings of nature.

Have you ever considered the metaphorical significance of spring? Many of us have endured the winter phases of our lives for extended periods. It is time to embrace our personal spring. For some, this season represents the perfect moment to bring ideas to fruition. If you've harbored dreams and aspirations for ages, wondering when to realize them, now is the time—this is your spring. Step outside your comfort zone and enter the garden of life, where ideas are planted and nurtured until they flourish.

There's no need to overanalyze the timing; perfection is less important than action. Simply recognize that it is spring and seize the opportunity to sow the seeds of your aspirations. The rain will certainly come. I am someone who believes in action overriding dreaming and imagining. While great things start with ideas, these must be nurtured into reality. Without action, imagination remains a daydream.

Proceed confidently with whatever good you intend to achieve. Give your ideas, plans, goals, projects, or undertakings the chance to materialize. Permit positive relationships, charitable deeds, community service, and acts of love to flourish. Life is created through the act of sowing and sustained by nurturing growth. Do not let your potential remain dormant. Proper stewardship involves planting and nurturing your seeds to vitality.

Recall that those who plant nothing should expect to harvest nothing. As Audrey Hepburn said, "To plant a garden is to believe in tomorrow." By sowing your ideas, allowing them to germinate, and carefully nurturing them with actions, you ensure an abundant harvest. The world eagerly anticipates the fruits of your efforts. Your productivity will naturally attract those who appreciate your offerings.

Don't Say It Won't Work

I can assert with confidence that experience is one of the greatest obstacles to innovative thinking. This is not to say experience doesn't have its merits. Often, individuals are assigned specific roles due to their seasoned expertise. Organizations typically avoid placing rookies in sensitive or critical positions because they might not have acquired the necessary experience. However, this very experience can impede creativity and innovation. It often leads us to rely on conventional methods rather than thinking outside the box. When a well-experienced and highly regarded professional states, "That won't work," it is usually based on their experience, not on a creative or innovative thought.

In childhood, you believed many things were possible. You might have imagined your father could buy you a small hot air balloon to take you to the moon. Such belief stemmed from a lack of life experience and the facts that would later make you know otherwise. As we age and accumulate experience, our imaginative capacity and the mindset that everything is achievable diminish. I explored this extensively in my book, *Pursuit of Personal Leadership*. Unless one continuously develops their imaginative abilities and engages in constant creative thinking, their experience will hinder them. This is why many corporate individuals struggle to envision change and to drive innovation for the future. They often dismiss ideas with "That won't work."

One of my core philosophies is never to declare something unworkable until I've tried it in multiple ways. People often label things impossible due to narrow-mindedness. We must cultivate a mindset inclined toward exploring possibilities, irrespective of our extensive knowledge and experience. In both personal and professional spheres, refrain from saying and believing, "It won't work." As Jesus Christ said in Mark 9:23 (NIV), "Anything is possible if a person believes." Begin to accept that incredible things are doable. However, mere belief is insufficient; one must also be willing to act, embracing ambiguities along the way.

When I started learning science in elementary school, the concept of hypothesis was particularly striking. Many groundbreaking discoveries began as assumptions, with someone curious enough to theorize, venture into the unknown, and build upon their speculations until they reached revolutionary conclusions.

Achieving anything remarkable requires a degree of ambiguity. Consider this: if all answers were already known and no risks were involved, then everyone would achieve great feats. Why is it that not everyone accomplishes extraordinary things? The simple reason is that all great achievements entail taking chances.

Do you find yourself needing to know whether something will succeed before starting it? Are you overly cautious about making mistakes? Do you sometimes hesitate to embark on something big because you're uncertain of its success? You're not alone. One way to determine whether something will work is by trying it. Again, refrain from declaring something unworkable unless you've tried it repeatedly in different ways. ***Great achievers embrace ambiguity.*** There are numerous paths to groundbreaking achievements, but without the willingness to try, we cannot achieve anything significant.

Those who attempt stand a chance; those who don't try have already failed. If failure is inevitable, let it occur while trying. Those who strive will learn, grow, and eventually succeed. Individuals who avoid risk and take no chances achieve little. Brian Tracy, author of over eighty books, aptly stated, "I've found that luck is quite predictable. If you want more luck, take more chances. Be more active. Show up more often."

The world seeks more doers, those willing to pursue their beliefs by taking chances. Your willingness to try and the experiences you gain through cycles of successes and failures will make you a remarkable individual.

Harness the Power of Light

Light supersedes darkness in all circumstances. No matter how pervasive the darkness, light invariably triumphs. You cannot extinguish light with additional darkness, but light can indeed dispel darkness. It is essential to grasp the true meanings of both light and darkness. Darkness can be simply defined as the absence of light. This analogy compels us to reflect on our own lives, success, and fulfillment in the context of light and darkness. Ignorance operates similarly to darkness: an unilluminated mind is shrouded in darkness, or ignorance.

You might then ask, "What constitutes light?" The answer lies in learning and acquiring knowledge that enlightens the mind. Those who consistently achieve success have enriched their minds with pertinent information. Knowledge stands as the remedy for ignorance; just as darkness signifies the absence of light, ignorance equates to the absence of knowledge. To overcome ignorance, one must exhibit humility and a willingness to learn and grow. In today's world, there is no excuse for remaining ignorant when vast amounts of information are readily accessible, often without cost.

However, a pervasive trap exists—some individuals remain ignorant without realizing it. They mistakenly believe they possess knowledge, yet they lack true understanding. Such individuals assume leadership roles, run businesses, and make societal decisions without being informed. How can one lead or manage without proper knowledge? In all endeavors, we must commit to operating in the light and acquiring necessary knowledge. Ignorance is not helpful; it serves as a metaphorical blindfold. Being unaware blinds one and keeps them from understanding what is unknown. Embrace enlightenment to avoid stumbling through life's journey. As the saying many have uttered as far back as Confucius goes, "It is better to light a candle than to curse the darkness."

Why is walking in the light of knowledge so crucial? Because knowledge unlocks freedom. *Those who are knowledgeable evade the oppression that ignorance brings.* Enlightened individuals can guide others, demonstrating pathways to liberation. When people recognize that you possess knowledge that can emancipate them, they are naturally drawn to you. Through your knowledge, you can illuminate others' paths and break the cycle of ignorance.

Be Cautious of How You Think About Others

Whenever I observe a bustling street and see people passing by, attending to their daily routines, I try to imagine what is on their minds. They are likely contemplating work, family, hobbies, friends, personal growth, financial challenges, or even basic survival. People are often absorbed in the trials and triumphs of life.

While some may be plotting harmful actions, most individuals are pursuing positive goals, simply minding their business and striving to make life work. However, we naturally tend to think less favorably of others, perceiving them as different or making unwarranted assumptions about them.

How we think about others is significant. Our expectations shape our perceptions. Often, we form opinions about people before meeting them based on our thoughts rather than their actions. Our minds take the easy route, leading us to assume identities for others rather than trying to understand them better. We need to improve our outlook on other people and start viewing them more positively.

The essence of my point is this: it is beneficial to expect good things from those around us because our expectations shape our reality. If you anticipate goodness in someone, you are likely to find it. Conversely, if you expect negativity, you will notice their flaws, and regardless of their actions, you will focus on the negative aspect. As author Laura Ingalls Wilder said, "Persons appear to us according to the light we throw upon them from our own minds." Your perception of others is influenced by your mindset.

Instead of crafting fictional versions of people in our minds, we should concentrate on the potential collective good and appreciate others. People who value others are valued in return. Those who fail to see good in others seldom receive goodwill from them. When you value others, you attract exceptional individuals, and you draw resourceful people to you through your personal magnetism.

Focus on Key Issues

Have you ever worked with perfectionists who accept nothing short of their high standards? It is beneficial to maintain standards in our work, and it is crucial that we bring thoughtfulness, care, and sophistication to our tasks. However, it's equally important to channel our energy wisely.

Back in high school, I had classmates whose handwriting was neater and more legible than mine. Their notebooks were immaculate, their letters perfectly aligned. These classmates dedicated significant effort toward crafting notebooks that resembled artistic masterpieces. However, the grades we earned in physics and math showed no regard for beautiful handwriting. One could embellish their math homework artistically, but it wouldn't change the fundamental principles of math. My focus was on comprehending these principles rather than excelling in creating aesthetically pleasing notes in physics class.

Reflecting on this, I realize how often we can become engrossed in things that do not add value to our objectives. We sometimes waste time on activities that don't contribute meaningfully to our goals. Often, we fixate on minor details at the expense of more significant issues. The problem with focusing on trivial matters is the wasting of valuable time. We shouldn't engage in endless discussions without reaching decisions, nor should we rigidly cling to our viewpoints when numerous perspectives exist. Dwelling on past grievances instead of looking toward the future is a costly use of our time.

The essence of my message is this: distinguish between the essential and the nonessential in all your endeavors. Identify what is critical to achieving your goals and separate it from what isn't. Learn to release petty, insignificant concerns and focus on key, necessary activities. As Alvin Toffler, businessman and futurist said, "You've got to think about the big things while you're doing small things, so that all the small things go in the right direction." We must ensure our efforts align with our overall goals.

Many struggle to achieve remarkable outcomes because they major in the minor. Creativity and innovation suffer when we expend energy on inconsequential matters. Given the fact that we will always have limited time every day, there's little room to squander our time on irrelevant tasks.

For instance, throughout this book, I have highlighted personal development and growth as a primary pathway to mastering personal magnetism. Focusing on self-improvement naturally attracts people to us. Conversely, prioritizing efforts to please others over personal growth constitutes majoring in the minor. It's time to concentrate on what truly matters, such as activities that bring us closer to realizing our vision. Don't squander your chances on minor issues when major tasks remain unfinished. It's futile to persuade others to support us by trying to please them when addressing problems effectively will naturally draw them to our side.

CHAPTER 6 SUMMARY

Creativity and innovation are essential for problem-solving and progression. They let us challenge the status quo and turn our dreams into reality. Here are the key points from this chapter.

1. Finding new horizons
   - Many people have unfulfilled dreams because they are held back by temporary obstacles. It's essential to seek new opportunities and take action to move beyond comfort zones.

2. Developing a strong and insightful mind
   - Engaging in meaningful conversations and thinking like one with a great mind rather than focusing on trivial matters is crucial. Great minds operate on the level of ideas, which leads to significant achievements.
3. Remembering the metaphor of spring
   - Spring symbolizes the perfect time to bring ideas to life. It's important to take action and nurture one's aspirations, much like planting seeds in fertile soil.
4. Avoiding the phrase "It won't work"
   - Experience can hinder innovative thinking. Instead of dismissing new ideas, it's important to explore possibilities and take chances to achieve great things.
5. Harnessing the power of light
   - Knowledge dispels ignorance and leads to enlightenment. Acquiring and sharing knowledge helps overcome limitations and attracts others seeking guidance.
6. Thinking positively about others
   - How we perceive others shapes our interactions. Expecting good in people can lead to positive outcomes and build valuable relationships.
7. Remember to focus on key issues.
   - It's crucial to prioritize important tasks and avoid getting bogged down by minor details. Personal development and growth should be the primary focus to achieve significant results.

CHAPTER 6 REFLECTIONS FOR ACTION

It's time to act on what you have learned in this chapter. Kindly read the reflection questions in the following table, and in the space provided, note what actions you will take and when.

	Reflection Questions
1	Is there a dream you haven't achieved yet? What's stopping you? Is something holding you back from reaching an important goal? What steps can you take to overcome it?
	Notes to self:
2	Decide not to participate in trivial conversations and aim to think and speak like one with a great mind. Can you distinguish between speaking ambitiously and being boastful? Is the difference clear?
	Notes to self:
3	When confronted with an idea that appears too ambitious to be feasible, how do you react? Do you take time to consider it or dismiss it outright? Be honest with yourself. Commit to reshaping your mindset toward imagination and creative thinking. Resolve to find ways to make things work rather than automatically assuming they are impossible.
	Notes to self:
4	Perform an internal assessment to verify whether you have been leading or functioning without adequate knowledge.

	Identify any gaps in your information or understanding. Commit to acquiring accurate, reliable, and comprehensive information before making decisions. Implement this habit consistently.
	Notes to self:
5	Consider how you perceive others. Are you prone to making assumptions? Try expecting the best from those around you, whether they're your family members or coworkers.
	Notes to self:
6	It's crucial to evaluate your activities. Reflect on them and identify which are significant and which are trivial. Consider where you invest most of your time, on the major or the minor tasks. Commit to dedicating your energy, time, and resources to activities that advance your objectives, and eliminate trivial, unimportant tasks.
	Notes to self:

CHAPTER 7

BE AN OVERCOMER

You gain strength, courage, and confidence by every experience in which you really stop to look fear in the face. You must do the thing you think you cannot do.

~ Eleanor Roosevelt ~

This chapter delves into the connection between an individual's capacity to handle difficult circumstances and the persona they display. Those who aspire to cultivate personal charisma, earn the respect of peers, and possess an attractive quality that entices others must understand how to navigate their unique personal challenges.

How do you face life's challenges and seize its opportunities? Are you clear about your aspirations and know how to fulfill them? Do you possess a cheerful demeanor and strong faith in yourself and your ambitions? Do you know how to manage change and difficulty? Are you willing to learn from your errors and grow from your experiences? Are you committed to making a positive impact and contributing value to others?

If you've answered affirmatively, kudos! But if you find some of these questions challenging, don't be discouraged. Many individuals encounter difficulties and uncertainties in their lives, and sometimes they require and seek assistance and motivation to move past them.

Life is filled with a variety of challenges that test our strength and resilience. In this chapter, we will examine the nature of conquering such difficulties and the persistence needed to attain success. It is necessary to confront challenges directly and recognize that meaningful accomplishments require considerable work and sacrifice. Obstacles and setbacks often characterize the path to success, but these setbacks are crucial for learning and empowerment.

Here, we will consider different methods for addressing adversity, including keeping an optimistic mindset, being flexible, and remaining calm under stress. I intend to inspire you to have confidence in yourself and your capabilities, even against overwhelming odds. I will also emphasize the importance of taking actionable steps toward objectives rather than just hoping for success.

By the completion of this chapter, you will be reassured that no challenging time or setback is permanent. By using a proactive approach and applying knowledge from past trials, one can face life's hardships with determination. Success hinges on the capacity to adjust, stay goal-oriented, and keep a hopeful perspective despite the situation.

This chapter serves as a manual for improving one's value to others by tackling life's hurdles with tenacity and a positive outlook. It offers useful guidance and insights to support you in reaching your aspirations and surmounting barriers. Those who exert effort and persist through tough times can succeed and become people of impact and charisma. By engaging with this chapter, you will not only navigate the challenges and changes of life but also cultivate the charm that draws people to you and your mission.

Let's go!

Lean into the Challenges

Life presents us with diverse experiences; some are simple and others complex. In moments of ease, we operate normally without feeling pressured, and we enjoy the feeling of having control over our circumstances. Conversely, during tough or challenging times, our perceived control seems to diminish, leaving us disturbed, uncertain, or confused.

Indeed, life's journey resembles a continuous cycle of highs and lows. It is like a rollercoaster ride fluctuating between peaks and troughs. The path to success is far from smooth or flat; it's lined with obstacles, barriers, and crossroads that each person must encounter. The way we traverse this landscape is crucial, but facing challenges is an inevitable aspect of everyone's quest for success. The pivotal inquiry remains: How do you respond to hardships?

Merely sitting idle, indulging in pessimism, and succumbing to despondency when faced with adversity won't alter the prevailing conditions. Figuratively burying one's head in the sand won't equate to reaching the shore. Most times, you must confront dire circumstances with determination and stand firm against adversity. While this may seem straightforward, it is essential to recognize that confronting challenges is not easy; it's a choice between prevailing over them or being overwhelmed by them.

In times of crisis, those around you scrutinize your response. Your approach to handling pressure and adversity, regardless of its nature, reveals much about your character. I have observed that individuals tend to gravitate to those who strive to endure hardships rather than those who get overwhelmed easily. Indeed, resilience and maintaining composure are traits that attract influential people.

Consider the scenario of attempting to unlock a door by trying multiple keys in a set of twenty-five. The probability of success in the first few attempts is slim, yet persistently trying more keys increases the likelihood of finding the correct one. Similarly, in life, we might find ourselves just beginning our attempts at success, and perseverance may be required until the right key is found.

Reflect on your current situation. Every path to success involves inevitable hurdles, all of which demand readiness to face and surmount. Achieving our aspirations calls for sacrifice, risk-taking, and enduring unpleasant circumstances. Committing to overcoming these challenges is vital.

Surrendering too swiftly, shying away from difficulties, opting for the path of least resistance, and retreating when faced with obstacles are unattractive qualities. For instance, when assembling a team for a task, you'd likely select someone exuding positivity, resourcefulness, and a problem-solving orientation. Opportunities favor those inclined to address challenges over those who embody them. There is no merit in showcasing weakness in both attitude and work ethic. Rather than recoiling, we should endeavor to lean into the challenges we face.

Achievements of high value seldom come with ease; it is through overcoming adversities that we meet our objectives and fortify ourselves. This appeals to those who value our strength. Success lies beyond the proverbial river, requiring persistent effort to attain the opposing shore. Should you possess a dream or noble goal, do not abandon it due to trials. Each conquered challenge not only draws you nearer to your goal, but also enhances your appeal to others. By honing your ability to navigate through difficulties, you inevitably place yourself in a favorable position among those who acknowledge your significance.

Pay the Price for the Prize

Freetown is a charming historic capital city in Sierra Leone, West Africa. One might assume from its name, "Freetown," that things come without cost, but this isn't true. Why then do some believe that valuable items should be free?

Everything of value comes with a price. Anything received for free has either been paid for by someone else or holds no real value. Take a moment to consider if anything of worth has ever been acquired for free.

Athletes, perhaps more than most, understand the concept of paying for success. Those winning medals at the Olympics have spent countless hours training, pushing their limits to break records and earn their awards. The journey of life is similar; we invest effort to gain rewards. It's also apparent that the greater the investment, the more significant the potential return.

Achieving personal success means contributing our utmost efforts. The output of our lives' endeavors will be commensurate with our level of input. Exceptional achievement requires substantial effort. Should your goal lie at a peak, you must endure the climb to reach it.

Numerous illustrious individuals have paved the way to a better world through their sacrifices. We reap the benefits left by pioneers—advocates of freedom, innovators, artists, educators—and those who've revolutionized our world through their contributions and sacrifices. Such individuals possess an attractive force: the power of personal magnetism.

The truth remains: those seeking giveaways and discounts, who focus on receiving rather than giving, often lack personal appeal. In contrast, there's an irresistible charm in those who give selflessly despite the challenges they face. "Success never goes on sale. Be willing to pay the market price," said author Randy

Gage. Contemplate what you're willing to invest in for your own goals. What sacrifices will you make for the betterment of humanity and others around you? A commitment to humanity inspires trust and draws others near, building profound connections in marriage, family, work, friendship, and community.

Conquer Your Brick Wall

Our journey through life is marked with a variety of experiences that can be uplifting or challenging. The good moments seem to flow smoothly, while the rough times can make us question the value of our endeavors. Overcoming setbacks is hardly straightforward. If you've ever given your all for a significant pursuit only to hit a dead end, you'll appreciate what I am saying. Our reaction to setbacks can either spur growth or lead to discouragement.

Pursuing meaningful goals inevitably leads to encountering obstacles. The most easily attained goals are often the least valuable. *If the path was easy, it would be crowded with travelers.* History shows us that successful ventures have often endured rigorous tests and faced numerous challenges along the way. These challenges are like the valley of death, where aspirations and plans falter and dreamers sometimes give up. This valley can appear at any time during our endeavors, posing insurmountable gaps to leap over or walls to break down.

Yet one fact remains: no tough period or disappointment lasts forever. *Tough Times Never Last but Tough People Do* was the title of Robert Schuller's 1983 book. We grow stronger through our experiences. Echoing Steve Harvey's words, "In every failure, there is both a lesson and a blessing." It's essential to seize these lessons and blessings as failure is not the end.

Disappointments offer a chance to refine our actions using the insights gained. Though outcomes may sometimes deviate from our expectations, adopting a broader perspective helps us find meaning in confusing circumstances. As Napoleon Hill, author of *Think and Grow Rich,* once said, "Every adversity, every failure, every heartache carries with it the seed of an equal or greater benefit."

Many people don't conquer their metaphorical brick wall because they lack suitable strategies and tools. When confronted with such a barrier, several routes are available: climb over it, break it down, find a different path, or succumb to inaction. How will you respond?

We must persevere in our quests despite difficulties, pondering on how to surpass them before translating those thoughts into action. Sometimes the key lies in adopting an attitude that acts like a sledgehammer against barriers or in the resilience to scale them. Alternative paths should also be considered, and seeking assistance from others might be necessary.

Are you experiencing hardship in your professional or personal life? Persist in moving forward, leveraging these encounters for learning and growth. Our reactions during trying times shape our character. To offer yourself as a gift to the world, mastering the art of conquering challenges is a must. The value we add stems from the experiences we accumulate in difficult situations; they contribute to your unique offering to society.

Remember, no circumstance is permanent. Change is constant. Despair should never be an option. Keep your eyes fixed on the potential lessons and blessings and recognize the opportunities ahead. Heed Eleanor Roosevelt's advice: "You gain strength, courage, and confidence by every experience in which you really stop to look fear in the face. You must do the thing you think you cannot do." The fact that those who keep moving forward in the face of adversity possess a charm that inspires others cannot be overemphasized. People generally gravitate to our strengths and not to our weaknesses although both are intertwined.

Against All Odds, Be a Believer

It is commonly argued that having no expectations prevents disappointment, with the rationale being that without anticipation, disappointment is impossible. This idea may sound reasonable on the surface, but it contradicts a fundamental tenet of achievement. The absence of expectations often leads to a lack of action and ultimately, nonachievement. Expectations fuel belief in the seemingly unattainable. It's well-acknowledged that Neil Armstrong and Edwin Aldrin expected to set foot on the lunar surface, and that came to fruition on July 20, 1969.

Our actions as human beings revolve around the framework of expectations and the conviction that future events or outcomes will occur, despite their current intangibility. This principle underlies your dedication to your job with the assurance of remuneration, your investment of capital with the hope of gain, and even the simple act of going to bed with the intention of waking up after a few hours.

However, we sometimes find ourselves hard-pressed to nurture optimistic expectations or believe in positive outcomes, particularly when circumstances prove challenging. Common societal influences, coupled with past personal experience, often discourage us to the extent that we set our sights low and keep our dreams modest, letting negativity pervade and grand expectations and aspirations be curtailed.

Reflect upon humanity's most significant achievements; they were accomplished by those who had unwavering belief in the face of adversity. The adage, "Seeing is believing," is popular, yet it can be contended that "Believing is seeing." Without belief, achievers see nothing; to achieve tangible accomplishments, belief must precede actualization.

Those who insist on visual proof of the destination before embarking on a voyage might as well not embark at all. In contrast, visionaries perceive the end goal with their minds' eye, filled with expectation and belief in their ability to realize their objectives. Significant endeavors demand an element of faith. Employing imagination and the confidence in eventual triumph is crucial because beliefs and actions shape our reality.

Our beliefs are the drivers behind our actions. Without belief, effort is unlikely, yet when faith takes root and propels someone toward a cause or venture, they become indomitable. Are you among the unstoppable?

To harness energy and motivation for remarkable feats, a firm belief in the goal is essential. Success in any endeavor is contingent upon true conviction. Those with sincere devotion to their chosen pursuit demonstrate commitment and subsequently reap the rewards.

Often, we must maintain belief against formidable odds. You may encounter dissent or hardship, and your activities might be misunderstood by others who may even object. However, if you're convinced about your path, persevere in faith and trust in your ultimate success.

The world awaits the rise of more determined individuals. As Roy T. Bennett, author of *The Light in the Heart,* once said, "If you believe very strongly in something, stand up and fight for it." By being resolute in a noble pursuit, you draw positive attention. Results bring recognition and support to your cause and establish you as an influential figure within your sphere as you act with great expectations.

The Worst-Case Scenario Is Not Your Scenario

I approach statements of realism with caution as they are occasionally a mask for pessimism. Acknowledging realism is valid, yet it often seems we oscillate between being optimistic realists or pessimistic realists. Which one resonates with you?

Do you habitually anticipate negative outcomes, always thinking about all the possible failures? Perhaps you have experienced someone in a strategy session who quickly points out flaws without proposing constructive solutions. I hope this doesn't describe you. It is prudent to identify risks and potential threats that may derail our undertaking. Managing risks effectively should be part of our approach to success. However, risk management should not degenerate into outright negativity, making us focus on failure rather than opportunities.

History's overachievers didn't dwell on reality; they targeted possibilities. If you're waiting to see everything fall into place before beginning your endeavor, you might never initiate action.

Envisioning an ideal outcome—the overarching goal that propels us forward—is crucial. Why fixate on an undesired endpoint? Constructive visualization should guide your journey. Remember, the scenes you imagine tend to determine your path toward reality. Avoid images that veer you off course.

Despite knowing we must face life's truths and barriers, let's not get sidetracked from our primary goals. Focusing only on the worst-case scenario and the negative—as though it's prudence—often leads to defeat. Success is born from mindset; individuals' achievements and outcomes arise from their mental perspectives.

Aspiring for greatness requires sustained optimism and a firm belief in possibilities. Napoleon Bonaparte famously remarked, "Impossible is a word to be found only in the dictionary of fools." Barriers are surmountable with the right mindset.

The future you seek must first be envisioned and extend to how you perceive your role among others. Are you among world-shapers? Do you confidently believe in your capacity for greatness, or do you default to expectations of failure or misfortune?

It is time to release yourself from thoughts of pessimism, discarding any version of events that only fixates on what could go wrong without a constructive way of finding opportunities. Focus on what can be achieved and the good that can follow. Dream big and accomplish big. When your dream is big enough, you position yourself to attract those who believe in it to help you achieve it.

When Change Happens to You

It's often said that change is the sole constant in life, persisting regardless of our actions or inactions. It stands as one of the essential axioms of existence and is unavoidable.

But change isn't just a random occurrence. We can influence certain aspects of it even if much remains beyond our grasp. This necessitates an appropriate mindset toward change. The reality is that control isn't always ours to wield. Despite diligent planning, precision, and competence, successes and failures are both part of living.

Many experiences come from others' choices and behaviors; we have no direct influence over this. Our power doesn't extend to the personal decisions of others. We're subject to unexpected events as a result. For instance, someone could walk out of your life, propelled by their pursuit of something better or for countless other reasons, and you would have no control over that.

Likewise, others often make critical decisions about us. Whether job hunting, vying for a promotion, closing a business deal, or seeking someone's hand in marriage, these are instances where another's decision plays a role. Acknowledging that external conditions can shape our circumstances is vital. We should be willing to adapt our attitude when facing changes not of our making.

Our response to change is typically observable by those around us. Your conduct when things fall short of expectations is telling. What's crucial is our response to life's changes.

Moreover, we exert no control over variables such as natural occurrences, weather, or governmental policies. It's fruitless to lament poor weather; rather, we should adjust our outlook and anticipate the day's potential.

Adapting to change occupies a considerable portion of our lives. Thus, evaluating how well you cope with it becomes pertinent. Do you maintain a positive mindset toward change, adapting as you go along? Experiencing change, whether positive or negative, is natural, yet dwelling on the negative is unproductive. Rather, we must constantly pivot toward new strategies and behaviors. Author Mandy Hale poignantly stated, "Change is painful, but nothing is as painful as staying stuck somewhere you don't belong."

The observation that the most prosperous individuals recognize the three forms of change—inevitable changes outside of our control, reversible changes, and proactive changes we can initiate—holds true. When change transcends your influence, it's classified as inevitable—your task then is to adapt.

Adapting effectively to change starts with an attitude adjustment. Without the correct mindset, unavoidable changes can feel insurmountable. Fostering resilience and flexibility is key when faced with change, instead of succumbing to defeat. By mastering adaptation to change, you cultivate a character that enhances your appeal and draws others closer.

Don't Lose Your Head over It

A mark of personal leadership maturity is the ability to remain composed in the face of distress, disorder, or difficulties. If you find yourself frequently overreacting when pushed to the brink, it's time to reassess your emotional intelligence and devise a growth strategy. Respect from others often eludes those who cannot manage basic interpersonal issues with a level head. To cultivate an aura of personal influence, one must consistently demonstrate poise and stability.

Every day we encounter situations that can upset our balance. It might be someone's words or actions or the sense of being treated unfairly. We may face others' decisions that affect us and we disagree with. We may be met with harsh treatment, provocations, or outright challenges. These moments are prime opportunities to exhibit true personal leadership and maturity.

It's important to understand that losing control only serves to complicate issues rather than resolve them. A negative emotional explosion has never been known to effectively solve a problem. What kind of disposition do you have? A quick-tempered nature will cause others to keep their distance due to your potential unpredictability and associated risks. Indeed, *unmanaged tempers have often been the catalyst for regrettable decisions.*

Maintaining a cool, calm, and composed demeanor enables us to better understand our environment and make calculated, thoughtful decisions. Coauthor of *Chicken Soup for the Soul,* Jack Canfield, once said, "You only have control over three things in your life—the thoughts you think, the images you visualize, and the actions you take."

One particularly harmful outcome of losing composure is making poor choices. Decisions arrived at during emotional upheaval tend to lack sound judgment. Often, the most impulsive and irrational actions arise when pure emotion displaces rational thought.

Are you aware of what pushes you to the limit? Recognizing these triggers is crucial to enhancing self-control. We are charged with the duty of transforming disorder into orderliness. Regardless of external circumstances, maintain your composure. Command the situation. By mastering this, you'll attract the best companions and colleagues, thereby mastering the art of personal charm.

Disengage From the Wishers' Circle

Only a minuscule proportion of the almost eight billion people on earth will do something truly grand or spectacular in their lifetime. The majority might have wishes but accomplishing them is another story. Take financial wealth, for instance; many aspire to financial success, yet there is a significant disparity between those who desire wealth and those who attain it. Likewise, grand achievements don't materialize by merely wishing. No one attains greatness solely through their desires.

The explanation is straightforward. Remarkable accomplishments aren't simply handed out. Those aiming for noteworthy success need to break free from the complacency of wishful thinking without action.

Your grand aims and creative ideas must be matched with concrete steps. Yearning for exceptional things is not enough; you must resolve to obtain them and demonstrate this through definitive actions. Instead of waiting for freebies, start formulating a tangible action plan.

Ultimately, people are drawn to the fruits of your efforts. No matter how much you speak of your own virtues, without tangible results, you won't earn respect or support. On the contrary, positive outcomes from positive actions can draw admiration and confidence from others.

Consider how this book was once just an idea that took action to realize. Dreams, visions, imaginations, ideas, or intentions remain as such until acted upon. Change and creation come exclusively through proactive steps; if nothing is done, nothing changes.

It's not wishful thinking that brings about significant achievements, but the commitment, hard work, and actions of those daring to defy the odds. Mario Cuomo encapsulated it best: "There are only two rules for being successful. One, figure out exactly what you want to do, and two, do it." It's time to step away from those who merely wish and associate with those who act. Only then can one witness transformation and earn the respect of others.

Do This When You Ride against the Wind

A couple of years ago, on a lovely afternoon, I chose to cycle to my friend's house a few miles away. It only took ten minutes to get there by bicycle, and I was thrilled by my speedy ride, feeling quite like a professional cyclist. However, the return trip took me three times as long. The reason? It was an exceptionally windy day. On my outbound journey, I hadn't noticed that the wind was at my back, aiding my speed, but I faced a headwind on the return, making cycling exceptionally strenuous.

Pedaling into the wind is tough and energy-draining. It seemed futile, with little gain for a significant amount of exertion. This mirrors the way some people channel their limited energy in nonbeneficial directions, working hard without obtaining substantial results. It raises the question, "Are we just fighting against the wind?"

Life is often compared to this struggle against the wind. While challenges and obstacles can be seen as the wind, not all hardships are detrimental. They may either obstruct our progress or help us soar higher, depending on how we respond to them. Each of us will face moments when we must confront these headwinds, and our reaction to adversity reveals a lot about our character.

In truth, while some capitalize on difficult circumstances to make progress, others may succumb to despair. Staying entrenched in failure is not appealing; nobody is drawn to associate closely with someone who has surrendered to defeat.

One might wonder then, how can we leverage this wind? Like the need for an airplane to adjust its attitude—the angle between its axis and the earth's horizon—to lift off the ground, we too must elevate our own attitudes to ascend amid life's gusty winds.

Instead of succumbing to life's trials, we must adopt a mindset that allows us to thrive through the turmoil. As Jimmy Dean put it: "I can't change the direction of the wind, but I can adjust my sails to always reach my destination." With the right attitude adjustment, one can rise above adverse situations and become a person admired and sought after by everyone.

Don't Let the Ebb and Flow Upset You

There's a town in Manitoba, Canada, called Ebb and Flow, situated next to a lake bearing the same name and with a population exceeding three thousand. I have fond memories of exploring the prairie area with my family, staying in cabins, visiting relatives, and enjoying Clear Lake, always passing by Ebb and Flow on the way. This unique town name, paralleling the natural pattern of the lake's water levels, triggers reflections about how life's journey is marked by continual progression and regression.

What does this metaphor imply? It suggests that our existence is characterized by fluctuations, like the natural ebb and flow of oceanic tides. There are moments when everything aligns perfectly, offering us a sense of achievement, joy, and fulfillment from our successes and the beneficial circumstances surrounding us. However, we all know that prosperity is temporary as high tides inevitably recede. Despite the joys we experience, most people find it challenging to accept the downturns, the retreats that invariably accompany life's peaks.

Yet as I mentioned earlier, it is vital to acknowledge that life inherently involves change, much like the perpetual movement of the ocean's tide. Rather than resisting or being distressed by these shifts, one should strive for composure amid the fluctuating tides of life. Anxiety during adversity solves nothing, particularly when factors are beyond our control. Steve Maraboli, author of *Life, the Truth, and Being Free,* once stated, "Life doesn't get easier or more forgiving, we get stronger and more resilient."

A sailor cannot command the wind, yet they can adjust their sails. *In the face of external circumstances outside our influence, we retain the power to modify our mindset and actions to reach our objectives.* The natural cycles of rising and ebbing tides mirror life's inherent ups and downs. Facing real-world challenges tests our strength, resilience, and commitment. When confronted with obstacles, it's essential not to be overwhelmed or toppled by life's turbulent waves. The world is looking for people who are imperfect but stable in the ebb and flow of life, those who will constantly adjust the sail until they bring everyone to the destination.

CHAPTER 7 SUMMARY

This chapter highlights the significance of surmounting life's obstacles to foster personal charisma, tenacity, and achievement. It offers guidance on cultivating a proactive attitude, adjusting to new circumstances, and implementing practical measures to accomplish one's aspirations using these keys:

1. Facing challenges head-on
   - Leaning forward and facing challenges with resilience and determination is essential. Resilient individuals who maintain composure during tough times attract others and achieve significant feats.
2. Mastering personal situations
   - To develop personal magnetism and command respect, one must first learn to master their own challenging situations and maintain a positive demeanor.
3. Adapting to change
   - Effectively adapting to change involves maintaining a calm attitude and being flexible, which enhances personal appeal and resilience.
4. Belief and expectations
   - Believing in one's goals, even against odds, fuels actions and ultimately leads to success. Expectations drive achievements by fostering a strong belief in positive outcomes.
5. Handling disappointments
   - Disappointments should be seen as opportunities for growth. Maintaining a hopeful perspective and learning from failures are crucial for long-term success.
6. Proactive steps
   - Success is achieved through proactive steps and hard work, not merely wishful thinking. Concrete actions are necessary to turn dreams into reality.
7. Emotional control

- Maintaining composure under stress is vital for personal leadership and influence. Emotional intelligence helps in making rational decisions and earning respect.
8. Resilience in adversity
    - Facing life's challenges with a positive attitude and resilience allows individuals to thrive and become influential figures.

CHAPTER 7 REFLECTIONS FOR ACTION

It's time to act on what you have learned in this chapter. Kindly read the reflection questions in the following table, and in the space provided, note what actions you will take and when.

	Reflection Questions
1	Consider your goals for the coming year. What personal commitments are you prepared to undertake to achieve them? Determine two places where you can contribute for the benefit of your family or community. Commit to these contributions.
	Notes to self:
2	What's your current situation? Are you facing a brick wall, with challenges and obstacles looming over your dreams or ideas? List three strategies to progress. Implement these strategies. Then consider helping someone else who is struggling to overcome their barriers.
	Notes to self:

3	Take a moment to reflect on your life's path. Consider your personal beliefs and expectations and commit them to writing. Contemplate whether these beliefs and expectations contribute to the greater good. If they fall short, consider how you might modify them. Begin to invest your energy into what you truly believe in. Maintain that belief, even through difficult times.
	Notes to self:
4	Is it time to shift away from negative thinking and embrace a more optimistic viewpoint? Consider your mental habits carefully. Decide to focus on the most positive outcomes when contemplating success. Recognize what's real but fill your thoughts with potential and opportunity. Cultivate a hopeful outlook.
	Notes to self:
5	Have you ever found yourself getting angry about a problem? Reflect on that incident. What insights did you gain? Consider three alternative actions to take instead of getting upset when you reach a breaking point. Document those strategies. Make a commitment to always consider your options carefully before taking any action.
	Notes to self:

6	Consider an important goal you aim to accomplish before the year concludes. List three actionable strategies to help you progress toward this objective. Implement the outlined actions. Proceed with determination.
	Notes to self:
7	Do you find yourself in ever-shifting circumstances? Maintain your concentration on your abilities and the final goal you aspire to achieve and keep your thoughts steady. Be in the company of those who uplift you. Cultivate positive thinking and speak affirmatively. Steer clear of surrounding negativity.
	Notes to self:

CHAPTER 8

BECOME AN EFFICIENT SELF-MANAGER

You don't have to be great to start, but you have to start to be great.

~ Zig Ziglar ~

Welcome to Chapter 8, where we embark on the journey of becoming efficient self-managers in the process of mastering personal magnetism. As I reflect on my experiences and the valuable lessons I've learned, I'm excited to share insights that can transform how we manage ourselves and our endeavors.

My story begins with a profound realization that taught me the importance of starting where you are and growing organically. Instead of leaping into vast commitments, begin with what you have, use it effectively, and gradually expand. This principle is crucial for sustainable success.

In this chapter, we will first explore the significance of intentionality. It's easy to fall into routines without deliberate thought, but true growth happens when we act with purpose. Whether it's our professional conduct, relationships, or daily habits, being intentional can make a significant difference. We'll delve into how to practice intentionality and reap its benefits now.

Additionally, we'll discuss the concept of having a Goal Positioning System (GPS): a clear sense of direction and purpose in life. Setting goals is not just about what we want to achieve but understanding why those goals matter. This clarity fuels our passion and keeps us motivated even when the journey gets tough.

We'll also touch on the importance of self-assessment and staying true to oneself. It's vital to evaluate our progress, remain humble, and acknowledge the support we've received along the way. Success is rarely a solo effort; it's a culmination of collective contributions. Recognizing this keeps us grounded and grateful.

Last, we'll consider the idea of returning to our home position: a place of rest and rejuvenation. In our quest for achievement, we must not forget the importance of taking breaks and caring for our well-being. Balance is key to maintaining long-term success and personal satisfaction.

As we navigate through this chapter, I invite you to reflect on your journey, embrace intentionality, set meaningful goals, and take care of yourself. Let's embark on this path to becoming efficient self-managers together.

Start Where You Are and Use What You Have

A few years back, an old friend approached me seeking my help to start his business in baby products. He requested a substantial loan to rent a large space and stock items, promising repayment from his sales profits. Despite the seemingly appealing proposition, I remained unconvinced. I pondered why he couldn't begin with a smaller amount, purchase a few items, sell them, reinvest the profits to buy more, and continue this cycle until his business expanded to his desired size. I also considered it might have been wise for him to approach a lender. He aimed to leap directly from nothing to success. Unfortunately, businesses do not operate this way. If he began as he proposed, without prior experience managing a business of that magnitude, he would almost certainly lose the entire investment.

The reason many people fail to succeed in their endeavors is not due to a lack of assistance but because they are reluctant to begin where they are and use the resources at their disposal. I've encountered individuals with impressive plans and proposals, some so compelling that one might be tempted to immediately commit resources to them. However, when individuals request a significant amount of money to start a venture, I always check to see how much they have accumulated on their own through hard work and how they plan to grow into the success they envision.

For example, if you excel at making shoes and have sold your first five pairs, that's excellent. The next step is to use the earnings from the sale of those five pairs to produce ten or twenty more, then strive to sell them. Don't worry if it takes weeks or months; make fifty more. If you find you can consistently sell fifty to a hundred pairs within a month or two, that may be the right time to consider setting up a small production system or a mini factory. The business will grow organically as you gain knowledge about the trade, market, economics, and most importantly, the discipline required for growth.

One potential mistake after learning to make shoes is to quickly approach a lender for a million-dollar loan to set up a shoe business. You might lose the money and get into trouble, not because you're a poor money manager but because you haven't yet learned to scale the business into the size you aspire to become.

If someone has not successfully managed $100, they are unlikely to manage $1,000 successfully. Instead of seeking what you don't have, why not start right where you are with what you have? Growing into your endeavor ensures sustainability; jumping into it may lead to failure. Use the resources you possess.

Salesman and author, Zig Ziglar, said, "You don't have to be great to start, but you have to start to be great." The authenticity you display and the growth you nurture in your business, work, or any other endeavor will attract the right people to your cause. Rapid success risks attracting the wrong people, whereas systematic growth ensures that you build genuine relationships along the way.

Always Make It Intentional

We often engage in many activities without giving them much thought, usually because they've become routines or habits over time. While there is nothing inherently wrong with routines as they can facilitate daily life, carefully crafted habits can be particularly advantageous. For instance, a student who habitually studies effectively is more likely to achieve academic success, just as an individual who consistently invests a substantial portion of their income is better positioned for financial stability.

However, one notable drawback of our routine-driven lives is the lack of intentionality. Many people simply follow convenient patterns rather than deliberately shaping their actions. Our potential to make meaningful changes depends on our readiness to act with purpose and foresight. Consider how you would meticulously plan your appearance, conversation, and behavior if you were scheduled to meet a high-ranking official such as a prime minister or president. Applying that same level of deliberate preparation to major aspects of life can yield significant results.

Achieving great things requires intentional effort; no one accidentally reaches the summit of a mountain. Significant accomplishments demand deliberate planning. Effective personal management involves setting clear goals and taking steps to realize them. As Steven Covey wisely noted, "The key is not to prioritize your schedule but to schedule your priorities."

Reflect on your work or business. Are you intentional about every aspect of your professional conduct? Leading a team or contributing to its success should be pursued thoughtfully rather than by merely routinely. Think strategically about how your actions impact results and what unique contributions you can make.

This principle extends beyond work into our families, relationships, community involvement, and associations. Purposefully cultivating these areas enriches our connections and service to others. It's crucial to intentionally decide how you present yourself to the world. Embrace an intentional approach to life and make deliberate choices that shape meaningful outcomes.

Use a Goal Positioning System

As each year ends and a new one begins, there is often a flurry of activity around setting new resolutions. Business-minded individuals establish goals to focus their efforts on specific, measurable achievements by year's end. Goal setting is critical for anyone who aspires to succeed. Without clear objectives or ambitions, success remains elusive. Living without goals is akin to navigating the seas without a destination. As Elbert Hubbard, author and philosopher said, "Many people fail in life, not for lack of ability or brains or even courage but simply because they have never organized their energies around a goal."

Contrary to common belief, goal setting is not an insurmountable task. It involves aiming to achieve something within a defined time frame. Your goal should incorporate the what, where, when, and how. What exactly do you want to accomplish? When do you intend to achieve it? Where will it take place? How will you go about it, and how will you measure your success? Goals should span various aspects of life, including career, health, finances, relationships, and spirituality. As author Bill Copeland rightly said, "The trouble with not having a goal is that you can spend your life running up and down the field and never score."

However, goals should not be set arbitrarily. When defining your goals, it's crucial to understand why you desire what you desire. Why did you choose this goal? What is the overarching purpose behind it? For instance, if your aim is to conquer Mount Everest this year, consider the reason behind it. If you aspire to attain a net worth of $25 million, ask yourself what the purpose is. Even the ambition to master personal magnetism and attract resourceful individuals to your circle requires introspection. Why do you seek influence and substance?

It's well-known that many who falter in pursuit of their goals often do so due to a lack of enthusiasm or waning passion. Passion diminishes when activities do not align with a compelling vision or dream. Enthusiasm generally flourishes when goals fit into a broader, more meaningful framework.

This brings to mind the necessity of a GPS for everyone. This GPS represents your ultimate life purpose or dream, which serves as a foundation for your goals. In my book, *Pursuit of Personal Leadership*, I discuss extensively how to uncover your life's purpose. Having a compelling reason behind your goals fosters the passion needed to achieve them. Update your GPS, set your goals, create a plan, and take action.

Be True to Yourself

I have a question for you: How are your goals for this year coming along? It's important to discuss goals regardless of the time of year. Each passing day should bring us closer to achieving them. Some of us may be successfully checking off items on our list, while others may feel like the year is slipping away without much progress. There are also those who experience ups and downs, making strides in some areas while struggling in others. What truly matters is moving steadily toward our objectives.

No matter your situation, it's vital to consistently review the goals set at the beginning of the year or season. Goals are not meant to be rigid; they can and should be shaped, updated, and refined. If you need to change direction, use this review period to decide. Progressing toward a meaningful destination is what counts, leading to fulfillment by year's end. Remember, setting no targets will guarantee hitting nothing. We must be proactive and intentional in our approach to life rather than letting life dictate our path.

Moreover, it's crucial to establish goals for our relationships. Consider how you can position yourself to earn favor and goodwill from those you meet. Continuously evaluate your progress honestly. Are you becoming someone people can trust and rely on? Many people remain unremarkable simply because they haven't aimed to be otherwise. Your plan should include strategies to attract the right people to your endeavors, and this needs regular assessment.

Achieving one's goals brings immense satisfaction and fulfillment. If you've ever reached a significant milestone, you understand this feeling. *Fulfillment often comes from actions taken with intention and for a greater purpose beyond personal gain.* As you reassess your goals, consider whether they will bring joy to you and benefit others. This is the moment of truth, a time to determine whether you will make a positive impact or live an average life.

Remain Calm

Sometimes achieving our goals depends on others' decisions and actions. Our ambitions may require input from other people. However, sometimes things don't go as planned, leading to frustration. Are you feeling uneasy because the opportunities you pursued didn't materialize? You're not alone. Many of us find ourselves seeking assistance, trying different approaches, and exploring various options.

It can be tough to handle the disappointment of hearing "No" from places where we'd hoped for positive outcomes. We often wonder why it's difficult for someone to lend a hand, especially when we believe they have the means to help. I've faced this situation many times and understand it can be painful. Giving up might even seem easier than persevering. This recalls a quote I recently encountered: "Anyone can give up, it's the easiest thing in the world to do. But to hold it together when everyone else would understand if you fell apart, that's true strength." Although the author is debated, this quote resonates with me.

Here's some good news: don't be disheartened if you didn't receive help as expected. If someone promised something but then withdrew, don't let it bother you. If someone chooses not to assist you, it means they weren't meant to be your support. Not every opportunity is meant for you. When you find the right one, it will open for you.

Stay calm; help is on its way. We cannot afford to give up in the face of rejection. Hearing "No" allows us to move forward and explore new paths. Keep asking, seeking, and knocking until you find and receive what you need. The person or people who will help you bridge the gap from where you are to where you are meant to be are nearby. Keep your eyes open, stay hopeful, and continue your efforts. You will reach your destination.

If you have ever waited a long time for something and finally achieved it, you know the satisfaction and fulfillment it brings. So don't lose heart now. Stay encouraged. Remain calm. Maintain a positive outlook on yourself and your circumstances. Things will change, and you will eventually celebrate. The help you need will come.

Don't Wait for the Perfect Timing

Can anyone truly time something perfectly? If you can, you must possess clairvoyance. The perfect time is an elusive concept that never materializes. Those who wait for it might end up waiting indefinitely. You don't need to wait for everything to align with your goals or ambitions before you take action. Many have spent a significant amount of time doing just that.

While there may not be a perfect time to do something, there certainly is the right time. The ideal time to plant a tree might have been twenty years ago. If you didn't do it then, the next best time is now. If you are trying to hunt a deer in the forest, assuming it is legal where you live, the right time is when you first get a clear view. Waiting for a more perfect moment could mean missing your chance.

Many people miss opportunities by waiting for the perfect timing. They forget that a farmer who focuses too much on minor weather details will never plant seeds. A farmer plants when the season is right; he does not wait for perfection. As author Holly Lisle aptly said, "If you have dreams you want to pursue, the time is now. There is no perfect time, and there is no better time. There is only the time you lose while you're making excuses."

What season are you in? Is it your planting season? Then go ahead and plant. There is no perfect time to start a business, build a family, attend school, learn a trade, write a book, hone a skill, change a habit, or undertake any worthwhile endeavor. When it's the right season, move forward without waiting for perfection.

Why is this important? Perfection is unattainable. Often, repeated efforts are necessary to find success. Many times, we simply need to take a step of faith, hoping things will work out. If they don't, we try different approaches. People might not always support your plans, even those you trust. If you have found something meaningful and you're passionate about it, go ahead and pursue it. Waiting for others' approval has led many to inaction.

Is there something you've wanted to do but haven't because the timing seemed off? You may need to take a step of faith. There is no perfect time; begin moving forward. Whatever you need to do, start now. Remember, to steer a car in a specific direction, it must first be in motion. A stationary car cannot be directed. Once you start, you'll find others with similar goals joining you. Success comes from moving forward, not from stagnation. Don't wait for perfect timing; keep progressing.

Don't Give Your Control to Anyone

Are you aware that many people around you have opinions about who you should be? This is why some individuals do not express gratitude when you help them; they expect it from you and are indifferent to how you feel afterward. It's the same reason you face blame when you fail: perfection is presumed. Thus, why did you fall short?

Indeed, those around you often have ideas about what you should do, where you should go, how you should dress, what you should say, whom you should befriend, what you should buy, and whom you should marry. You may seem to be the only one without this knowledge, but others believe they know. Many people live under the influence of someone who significantly controls their lives. Notice the use of the word "control." Some individuals cannot navigate life without adhering to the demands of others; that's giving your control away.

Early in my life, I learned to pursue independence. Although I learned from others and listened to their opinions, I strove to live according to my convictions rather than others' control or manipulation. Shouldn't the outcome of your life reflect your own beliefs and philosophy? Have you developed a personal philosophy grounded in knowledge, experience, and sound judgment? If so, you should not be swayed by external opinions. While opinions are plentiful, reasoning is rare. Those controlled by others often lack fulfillment as there is no satisfaction in merely living to please others.

We must recognize that cultivating personal charm and attracting others to us does not require pleasing everyone. You do not need to lower yourself to be loved or accepted by anyone. Being helped by someone does not make them your master. No one should have the power to dictate your thoughts and actions. You alone must take full responsibility for the course of your life.

It's time to assert yourself and exercise your freedom of thought and choice. Ultimately, only you are accountable for your life's outcomes. No one else bears responsibility for how things turn out for you. Researcher and author, Brené Brown, said, "If you own your story, you get to write the ending." Each person is responsible for their own decisions, actions, and outcomes.

At the same time, wise counsel holds much value. You may seek advice but ensure that you blaze your own trail. Do not surrender control of your life to anyone. Live with intention and deliberation, taking personal responsibility every step of the way.

Don't Ever Forget

You have probably heard the term "self-made millionaire." Many individuals are labeled as "self-made," but this term needs appropriate context. Can anyone truly build themselves up alone? Certainly, some people have faced many challenges, figuring things out as they navigated through life's difficulties. We admire the bravery of those who succeeded despite all odds.

Similarly, we commend those who had numerous opportunities, received help from various sources, and leveraged their fortunate circumstances to create something meaningful in life. Regardless, everyone who has made progress understands that they encountered helpful people along the way.

No matter how disadvantaged you believe you were or how much effort you think you invested single-handedly in your success, it is self-deception to think that none of your progress can be attributed to the support of others. There is nothing you possess that you did not receive, and those who offer help deserve recognition. As Calvin Coolidge said, "No person was ever honored for what he received. Honor has been the reward for what he gave." No solitary soldier forms a legion, no tree creates a forest, and no individual constitutes a crowd. Everyone receives assistance.

Before taking full credit for your achievements, consider the impact of those whose paths crossed yours during your journey. These could be family, friends, supervisors, colleagues, students, the community, or customers. Remember the times you relied on collaboration with others to reach your goals. Acknowledge the contributions of those who provided opportunities, advocated for you, supported you, stood by you, and believed in you.

There is a thin line between self-recognition and outright pride. Do not let ego consume you. It is wise to manage oneself by remaining humble about achievements, giving credit to those who extended their support. We must recognize those who deserve recognition and honor those who should be honored. Remember those who must be remembered. Let those who influenced you feel your gratitude. And if they cannot, let your humility set a new standard of success for the world to follow. Don't ever forget.

How Much Did It Weigh?

Scales are designed to tell us the weight of an item, which helps determine its value. For instance, gold may be measured in grams, meat in kilograms, and gravel in tons. Regardless of the unit used, a higher weight typically indicates greater worth.

However, weight isn't limited to tangible items. Intangible concepts can also be assessed by their weight. For example, how much does your idea weigh? You may weigh your options. You can be dealing with a weighty issue.

Now, let's consider one more nonphysical aspect: weighing your thoughts. We all desire meaningful results from our efforts. We want our hard work to result in tangible gains and rewards that satisfy us. *The outcomes in your life are inherently tied to the value of your thoughts.* Generally, individuals do not surpass the value of their thoughts. Typically, the results we achieve are proportional to the quality of our thinking. Therefore, it's crucial for everyone to evaluate their thoughts and ensure they are valuable. If your thoughts were measurable, would they hold significant value?

No matter the environment or opportunities presented, each person is constrained by the value of their thoughts. The way individuals manage relationships and opportunities often aligns with their thinking. I've observed that keeping great company and cherishing interactions with exceptional people heavily depends on one's self-perception. Like attracts like; if you think highly of yourself, you will attract equally remarkable people.

Our minds serve as powerful engines, controlling every action. Our thoughts and their nature influence what we do. If I believe I can climb a mountain, my mind will offer suggestions on how to reach the peak, forming the basis for my actions toward climbing it. Most of our behaviors are influenced by subconscious suggestions based on habitual thinking. Hence, having limiting thoughts isn't an option. We must ensure that our thoughts generate substantial value. Reflect on your own mind; assess your thoughts. What are their weight?

Return to Your Home Position

When I began studying the operation of industrial robots, I quickly learned that each robot has a home position. This home position is a specific spot in 3D space from which the robot starts and to where it returns after completing its tasks.

Similarly, humans also have their own home positions: places of peace and rest from which we embark on our daily activities and to which we should return afterward. Returning to this state of rest is crucial for rejuvenating and re-energizing ourselves for future endeavors.

However, it is troubling to see people who departed from their home position years before and did not return. They continuously pursue achievements, personal success, relationships, and other life goals without taking breaks. Like an old pendulum clock ticking away for ninety years, they neither slow down nor stop to rejuvenate, forgetting that humans are not perpetual machines; mental and physical breakdowns can occur.

A pertinent question to ask yourself is, "Is it all worth it?" Maybe it is, but we must balance our achievements with our capacity to achieve them. Have you ever felt extreme exhaustion leading to burnout? Are you currently feeling agitated, anxious, fatigued, or burned out physically or mentally? It might be time to consider if you have been working without returning to your home position.

The home position could involve activities like sleeping, taking a vacation, reading, spending time with family, or praying. Anything that helps you regain strength and vitality contributes to your home position. Pull back from overwhelming tasks, slow down, and return to your home position to rebuild vigor. The energy accumulated there will propel you toward your next goal. John De Paola said, "Slow down and everything you are chasing will come around and catch you."

Why is this important? We recognize that nobody in this world is indispensable. If you push yourself to the point of collapse, the world will keep moving without you. In everything you accomplish, remember to take care of your health, wellness, and mental stability. You are more valuable to those around you when you are healthy and mentally sound. Personal well-being significantly enhances your overall charisma. Maintain your health and prosperity by consistently returning to your home position.

CHAPTER 8 SUMMARY

This chapter focuses on becoming an efficient self-manager by emphasizing the importance of starting with the resources you have and growing organically. It highlights the value of intentionality in actions, setting clear goals aligned with your life's purpose, and regularly assessing progress to ensure meaningful outcomes. The chapter also underscores the significance of balancing work with personal well-being and acknowledging the support received from others along the journey. The key lessons can be summarized as follows:

1. Start where you are
   - Utilize the resources you currently have and grow incrementally. Jumping into large commitments without experience often leads to failure.
2. Be intentional
   - Deliberate planning and purposeful actions in all areas of life lead to meaningful outcomes. Routine activities should be done with clear intention.
3. Set goals with a GPS
   - Establish clear, actionable goals aligned with your life's purpose. Understanding the why behind your goals fuels passion and determination.
4. Be true to yourself
   - Regularly review and adjust your goals. Seek fulfillment through intentional actions that benefit both yourself and others.
5. Remain unperturbed
   - Do not be disheartened by rejection. Perseverance and continued effort will eventually lead to success.
6. Don't wait for the perfect timing
   - Act when the time is right rather than waiting for perfect conditions. Progress is achieved through continuous effort, not stagnation.
7. Don't give control to anyone
   - Live by your convictions and do not let the opinions of others dictate your life. Personal responsibility is key to true fulfillment.

8. Don't forget those who helped you
   - Acknowledge and appreciate the support received from others. Humility and gratitude foster stronger, more genuine relationships.
9. Weigh your thoughts
   - Evaluate the value of your thoughts as they shape your actions and outcomes. Higher-quality thinking leads to better results.
10. Return to your home position
    - Regularly take breaks to rest and rejuvenate. Balance between work and well-being is essential for sustained success.

CHAPTER 8 REFLECTIONS FOR ACTION

It's time to act on what you have learned in this chapter. Kindly read the reflection questions in the following table, and in the space provided, note what actions you will take and when.

	Reflection Questions
1	Visualize the scale at which you want your business or career to expand. Document this vision. Consider the gradual steps required to realize your envisioned goals. Assess what resources and assets you currently possess. Utilize these existing resources to begin your journey. Start from your present position.
	Notes to self:

2	Reflect on your daily actions to see if you act with purpose. Choose three areas where you can be more deliberate, such as your attire, words, diet, or a family relationship. Decide what and how you'll improve, then follow through.
	Notes to self:
3	Assess yourself to see if you have a GPS. If it is absent, begin a journey of self-discovery and vision. Start by asking, "What do I truly want to accomplish in life?" Establish clear goals and decide when you aim to achieve each one. Document them. After that, develop a plan of action. Outline how you will accomplish these aims.
	Notes to self:
4	If you have a goals sheet, take it out and review your goals. Update or refine them if needed. What steps will you take to achieve your goals? For each goal, decide what actions you will complete within a week. Then proceed with those actions. Imagine how you want the end of the year to look for yourself and your loved ones. What can you do today to make that happen? Act now.
	Notes to self:

5	Reflect on your current circumstances. Are there certain areas where you need to exercise calmness and patience after facing rejection? Consider offering support to someone, particularly in a professional or career context. Reach out and assist them. If you know anyone struggling with the disappointment of being told "No," share the insights you've gained from this book with them.
	Notes to self:
6	Reflect on your actions. Are they guided by your own beliefs, or are you just following what others think? It's up to you to decide. Strive to develop your own principles and values grounded in knowledge and reason. Then commit to living by them.
	Notes to self:
7	Consider the individuals who played significant roles in your success. List three to five people whose efforts were crucial for your achievements. If possible, contact them and express your gratitude. If that's not feasible, find an alternative method to recognize their contributions.
	Notes to self:

8	Evaluate your own thinking patterns. Do you think expansively or narrowly? Keep in mind that your thoughts influence your actions. Make a commitment to broaden your mindset; aim to think big and maintain positive thoughts about yourself and others.
	Notes to self:
9	Evaluate your pace to determine whether you are moving too quickly. Is there a need for you to slow down and take a moment to breathe? List three activities you can perform to create balance from your designated home position as outlined in this book. Proceed to complete these activities.
	Notes to self:

CHAPTER 9

BE PATIENT BUT PERSIST

The key to everything is patience. You get the chicken by hatching the egg, not by smashing it.

~ Arnold H. Glasow ~

Let us talk about the crucial art of patience and persistence. We live in an age where instant gratification is the norm, where the luxury of waiting is often seen as a burden rather than a virtue. Yet the true worth of anything valuable demands time and patience. As we navigate through various life stages, be it personal endeavors or professional milestones, the ability to wait with forbearance and act with steadfastness sets the foundation for lasting success and for making us the best we can be.

We often rush into decisions, driven by the urgency of the moment, only to realize later that haste can lead to failure. Patience is not a passive state but an active process of steady preparation. It enables us to harness our energies, to act with wisdom rather than impulse, and to maintain composure even when immediate results seem elusive.

Patience reflects our inner strength and self-control. It is the capacity to remain calm, to endure challenges, and to continue forward despite obstacles. This does not mean we become complacent or lethargic; rather, it means we focus on the journey, understanding that each step, each delay, and each setback is a building block for our ultimate goals.

In our moments of waiting, we are not idle. We are planning, preparing, and growing. This chapter encourages you to embrace those periods of anticipation, to see them not as wasted time but as opportunities to refine your strategies and enhance your resilience. When we patiently cultivate our dreams, we ensure that our actions are in harmony with our most profound goals, including becoming an influential individual and someone who radiates personal charm.

As we delve into the principles of patience and persistence, remember that every challenge you face is a lesson, every delay a chance for further preparation, and every setback a step toward your goals. Let us journey through this chapter with the understanding that while the path may be long and filled with trials, the persistence to stay the course and the patience to endure will ultimately lead us to our desired destination.

So, gear up for an insightful exploration into how patience and perseverance can transform your approach to becoming the person you are designed to be. Together, we will uncover the strength within to persist, the wisdom to wait, and the courage to continue, knowing that things are not falling apart but falling into place.

Wait for It

One of the toughest things to do is wait for something, especially when we don't know when it will happen. We're so accustomed to instant results that even a three-minute wait to heat our food in the microwave feels challenging. We crave quick outcomes and immediacy.

Here's the reality: anything truly valuable is worth waiting for. Seeking something worthwhile? Then practice patience. Don't rush into marriage, career choices, investments, or life decisions. Practice patience. Impulsive decisions and hastiness often lead people back to square one.

Does being patient equate to being slow, complacent, or unenthusiastic? Not at all. Patience signifies superior qualities like endurance and self-restraint while anticipating something significant or a change. Those who are patient maintain balance even under difficult circumstances. Are you patient? Do you lose your composure when things don't go your way?

Waiting patiently isn't synonymous with inactivity. The time we spend waiting allows us to prepare for what we anticipate. During this time, we act in faith of our future, aligning our actions with our expectations. Are you striving for something important? Do so with patience.

Patience is a virtue to nurture. Impatience is a flaw. The world needs more patient than impatient individuals—people who thoughtfully make decisions impacting future generations. As author Arnold H. Glasow stated, "The key to everything is patience. You get the chicken by hatching the egg, not by smashing it." In all your endeavors, be patient and learn to wait for the best outcomes.

Things Are Falling into Place Not Falling Apart

In my book, *Rip Off Your Blindfold*, I dedicated an entire chapter to encouraging those facing difficult situations. The chapter is titled, "Hitting Rock Bottom is a Good Thing." But how can an unpleasant experience be beneficial?

When we encounter challenging situations, we often experience stress and apprehension because we're unsure of the outcomes. Consider someone who loses their job or a loved one, becomes bankrupt or homeless, or is betrayed by someone they trusted. How could you explain to such an individual that their situation is beneficial?

Through my life's journey, I've realized that our perception during times of trouble or pressure is typically skewed. We focus solely on our problems and challenges, which clouds our understanding of reality.

Here is the truth: the experiences we endure prepare us for greater things. When we feel as though a situation is breaking us, it is actually shaping us. We become stronger not because someone instructs us to be strong but because we face circumstances that build resilience and strength within us. Often, when it seems like everything is falling apart, it is in fact falling into place. As songwriter Jeanette Coron said, "The greater the destiny, the greater obstacles you'll have to overcome. No great destiny comes without great challenges and sacrifices."

Consider grapes, which must undergo crushing and squeezing to become wine. A seed destined to grow into a plant must first be planted in the soil. *When you feel buried, you are simply being planted so you will grow into a tree that bears great fruit. You are submerged so you can emerge.*

During challenging times, focus on the lessons they bring. Allow the difficulties to fully transform you into a better version of yourself. You are on a purposeful journey. Stay the course, be an overcomer, and remember that things are falling into place, not falling apart. Be patient and let these transformations mold you into the best person you can be.

Keep Nurturing the Dream of Your Heart

As mentioned earlier, some people advise against having expectations to avoid feeling disappointed. However, I prefer to learn how to manage disappointments while still holding positive expectations in my heart. Don't let anyone dissuade you from having expectations. Why should anyone go through life without anticipating wonderful things?

Here's why maintaining great expectations is essential: expecting significant outcomes reflects your state of mind. Individuals with positive thoughts and a success-oriented mindset tend to have high expectations, so they achieve remarkable things. As Douglas H. Everett, chemist and author, said, "There are some people who live in a dream world, and there are some who face reality; and then there are those who turn one into the other."

Many people abandon their confidence and dreams due to past disappointments, which I understand. Yet if we don't nurture our dreams and believe in them, we won't take the necessary steps to achieve them. Don't allow anyone or anything to hold you back. You are closer to realizing your dreams than you might think.

Each day offers a fresh opportunity to pursue our dreams, so act with faith and move forward. Remember, if you don't believe in and nurture your own dreams, no one else will. You must expect your dreams to come true and show that belief by taking positive actions toward them. Be patient but persistent.

Now is the time to care for and protect your dreams, ambitions, and aspirations. Nurture those dreams until they grow into something meaningful. What dream are you nurturing? What vision do you have for yourself? Where do you envision yourself next? What mental edifice are you building? Keep thinking about these dreams and nurturing them with expectation until they become embedded in your subconscious mind. Positive circumstances will align with your efforts, and your dreams will become a reality.

Encourage Yourself in Your Change

Change is a fundamental part of life, and it's inevitable. It can be either positive or negative, but we all seek improvement. We desire our situations to get better and for things to change positively. Change is also a process. For example, we sometimes use tomatoes in paste form, which requires crushing tomatoes to make it. Similarly, iron ore must undergo high-temperature heating to extract steel. If your improved state is like tomato paste, you might have to experience crushing. Likewise, if your better situation resembles steel, you may need to endure the furnace. Significant improvements often come with a change process that involves some hardship.

When the change we wish for begins, we may not instantly see or feel the results. Often, we only notice the challenges, difficulties, hardships, or effort required for the change. This can be daunting. The key to staying committed is to focus on the anticipated outcome. The process is always worthwhile, and it's essential to accept the challenge and embed positivity in our minds.

We also need courage and, in most cases, must develop inner strength. Inner strength drives external actions. Nelson Mandela once said, "I learned that courage was not the absence of fear, but the triumph over it. The brave man is not he who does not feel afraid, but he who conquers that fear." We must conquer our fears, embrace courage, and face our situations bravely.

Where are you in your journey of change? You might be starting something new, trying to improve a situation, working toward a financial goal, or navigating a career shift. You could be in the challenging phase, feeling discouraged or worried about the outcome. My message to you is be courageous. Find encouragement within yourself during this change. Think about the satisfaction of achieving your vision, reaching your goals, attaining success, or completing your mission.

To move forward, you need courage, and you are the best person to motivate yourself. Let strength build within you. Embrace courage. Remember that you *can* achieve what you thought you couldn't. You become better through what you withstand and overcome. The process of being crushed and heated transforms you into the best version of yourself, making you more valuable to yourself and those around you. Encourage yourself as you go through your change.

Don't Pass the Buck but Own It

You might think this is straightforward, but for many people, it isn't. I've seen individuals blame others for something they did themselves. For instance, if you're driving and your car hits a pothole, you could either blame the municipality for not repairing the road or acknowledge that you could have avoided it with more caution. Both perspectives are valid. Similarly, you can hold your stove accountable for burning your food or fault the rain for causing a flood.

What doesn't come naturally is for us taking responsibility for our actions and attitudes. The worst thing we can do on our journey of self-improvement is pass blame to someone else without owning our part in the issue. As previously discussed, the key difference between someone who progresses in life and someone who doesn't lies in their attitude. Embracing personal accountability for our life's outcomes is an attitude we must learn and develop. The next time you're about to blame someone, consider your role first.

It's remarkable how some people with authority act vindictively. For them, when things go wrong, someone must be blamed and punished. They lack tolerance, always searching for someone else to fault instead of themselves. Often, vindictive individuals are responsible for creating the problem or environment that led to the issue, yet they refuse to accept responsibility. Rather than introspect, they prefer to make others suffer the consequences.

Before deflecting blame or punishing someone, ask yourself if you could have done something to fix the situation. Own it. Take full responsibility for your own life's outcomes. As newspaper columnist and editor Doug Larson said, "The reason people blame things on the previous generation is that there's only one other choice." That other choice is to blame ourselves so we can take responsibility.

To develop a personality that attracts others, you must learn to take responsibility. It's not just about assigning blame but about taking actions to solve problems instead of passing the buck. Owning situations, taking responsibility, and striving to make things right are rare qualities. Those who possess these qualities are usually valued as leaders, coworkers, partners, and collaborators. Conversely, those who constantly shift blame are often disliked, which limits their opportunities to succeed.

Don't Give Up on Anyone

You might not be formally titled as a leader, but if you have people who report to you or whom you coach, teach, or guide in any way, you are in a leadership role. One of the toughest aspects of leadership is to deliberately invest time and effort into others and maintain consistency in that investment until they mature. This becomes particularly challenging when working with individuals who lag significantly behind.

For instance, you might have a new employee still learning the technical skills necessary for their role. You may need to provide close guidance, watch them make mistakes frequently, consistently offer feedback on how to improve their work, and exercise patience as they learn. Many leaders tend to shirk their responsibility of nurturing others, preferring to work only with those who are already high achievers, forgetting that they too were once beginners.

While it's crucial to choose team members wisely, especially based on their capabilities, focusing on attitudes is even more beneficial. Individuals with the right attitude will learn and improve over time because of their positive mindset, while highly skilled individuals could be ineffective due to a poor attitude.

Throughout my experiences, I've observed that those willing to learn eventually grow and become valuable members of the team. Unfortunately, many so-called leaders lack the patience to identify potential in beginners and hastily label them incompetent.

Jack Welch, the legendary CEO of General Electric, said, "Before you are a leader, success is all about growing yourself. When you become a leader, success is all about growing others." As leaders, we should not abandon those we lead. We must consistently seek opportunities to be sources of knowledge, inspiration, and encouragement for our team members, which in turn helps us attract top talent. The most effective and appealing leaders are those who cultivate leadership in others.

Additionally, people differ greatly in their learning and growth pace. It's inappropriate to assess everyone by the same standards. If individuals are eager to learn and develop, it's a leader's duty to create an environment, provide the tools, and offer the support necessary for their success. Those who aren't useful today could very well become the superstars of your team tomorrow. Don't give up on anyone; they too will grow.

Don't Start until You Have Finished

Each new day, week, month, or year offers a fresh opportunity. Yesterday only holds power if we let it by refusing to progress. It's essential to leave behind where we've been and embrace the new opportunities each season brings. However, to truly harness today's potential, setting goals is crucial. The goals we outline for the future dictate the actions we need to take today.

I've never seen anyone achieve significant success without intending to do so. Remarkable accomplishments result from the deliberate desire, careful planning, and strenuous effort of those courageous enough to reach for greatness. It all begins with envisioning the endpoint, seeing where our lives can go through our mind's eye.

I mentioned three key elements: desire, planning, and effort. Success starts with the desire to achieve something specific, clear, and time bound. Identify your desires and write them down. When you specify desires, set timelines for achieving them, and develop measures to track them, they turn into goals. Do you have goals? What are you striving for? Document what you want to achieve in the future just as you envision it.

Next, create an action plan to reach those goals. Nobody builds a structure without first planning how to build it. Decide on the daily, weekly, and monthly steps to reach your goals.

What are steps one, two, and three for reaching your destination? Without a plan, a goal remains merely a wish. You must plan your path to achievement.

Then put in the effort—take action. Do what needs to be done. It's your actions, not your inaction, that bring you closer to your desired future. Remember, those who do nothing will gain nothing and become nothing. The process begins with a desire turned into goals, followed by a plan and actions.

The key is to finish before starting. Plan thoroughly for your day, week, and month before beginning them. Don't start the day until you have finished the previous one; don't start the week until you have finished the previous one; don't start the year until you have finished the previous one. Spend considerable time planning, put in the work, and watch your dreams materialize throughout the year.

Why is this important? The world currently suffers from a lack of visionary leadership. Few people dream of a better future for our world. Visions are scarce nowadays. If you are a visionary leader, you are among the most valuable and significant individuals globally. The world needs you. Your vision, planning, and actions will place you ahead of others, putting you in the company of influential figures rather than those of low cadre.

Slow and Steady Wins No Races

In children's fables, the saying, "Slow and steady wins the race," is a common figurative theme. The idea is that a slower but consistent and focused approach leads to achieving goals, emphasizing that there is no need to rush through life and that we should savor the journey. While it is true that you do need to take time to savor the journey, as I previously mentioned, it's crucial to acknowledge that life remains a race.

We shouldn't use the concept of "slow and steady" as an excuse for procrastination. We must recognize that we are in a race against time, with finite years ahead of us. Even those who live long lives may have only about a hundred years, which isn't an extensive period but is ample time to accomplish great things if we appreciate the value of time. Every moment wasted on delay and idleness is lost forever.

It's essential to develop consistent and productive habits on our path to success if we want to keep moving. Truly successful individuals tend to achieve their status through habitual discipline. Successful people are diligent and adhere to the principle of doing what needs to be done when it needs to be done. Whether in a sprint or a marathon, those who win races keep moving, and only the first-place finishers win. Everyone may complete a race satisfactorily, but medals are reserved for those at the top. Everyone has the power to choose their desired position in this race.

So, does slow and steady win the race? Perhaps slow and steady completes the race, but it doesn't necessarily mean victory. Immediate, consistent, and timely action is required. Do not postpone actions that can be taken today. Don't squander thirty hours on tasks you can complete in ten. Maintain your pace and don't slow down. Success requires speed, not haste, and on the road to success, there are no speed limits.

Whatever responsibilities you have, execute them swiftly and efficiently to make room for further accomplishments. Avoid a sluggish pace and keep advancing with the determination of a winner. As Charles M. Schulz said, "Life is like a ten-speed bicycle. Most of us have gears we never use." Strive to be both patient and quick and be persistent. Achieving success will attract others to you.

CHAPTER 9 SUMMARY

I wrote this chapter to help you navigate through challenges, cultivate patience, and stay focused on your ultimate goals as you grow in your journey to become a person of influence. Consider the following points to evaluate your past experiences, reflect on your current journey, and reignite your ambitions:

1. The importance of patience
   - Patience is essential for achieving lasting success. It involves steady preparation, inner strength, and self-control, which allows us to handle challenges calmly and wisely.
2. Active waiting
   - While waiting, we are not idle but planning and growing. This period helps us refine our strategies and enhance resilience, making our actions align with our profound goals.
3. Transforming challenges
   - Every challenge or setback is an opportunity to learn and prepare further. By staying persistent and patient, we can turn difficulties into stepping stones toward our desired outcomes.
4. Encouragement through change
   - Embracing change requires courage and inner strength. Focus on the positive outcomes and remind yourself that challenges shape you into a better version of yourself.
5. Personal accountability
   - Taking responsibility for our actions and outcomes is crucial for personal growth. Avoid shifting blame and instead work to solve problems, which fosters a respected and leadership-oriented personality.

6. Supporting others
   - Consistent investment in others' growth is vital. Recognize potential in beginners and provide the necessary environment and support for their development.
7. Vision and planning
   - Significant achievements stem from clear desires, careful planning, and dedicated effort. Envision your goals, create actionable plans, and take consistent steps toward realizing them.
8. Balancing speed and steadiness
   - Success requires a balanced approach of patience and timely action. Avoid procrastination, maintain a productive pace, and aim for consistent progress to achieve your goals.

CHAPTER 9 REFLECTIONS FOR ACTION

It's time to act on what you have learned in this chapter. Kindly read the reflection questions in the following table, and in the space provided, note what actions you will take and when.

	Reflection Questions
1	Reflect on your past experiences. Have you ever hurried into something that later didn't work out? What lessons did you take away? Consider your life path. Where do you need to practice patience? How can you approach things differently?
	Notes to self:
2	Assess your current situation. Are you facing difficulties? Choose to learn from them while staying focused on your

	goals. Identify three actions you can take to improve your circumstances and write them down. Remember, planning and correct action are crucial during tough times.
	Notes to self:
3	Did you have a significant dream that you no longer consider? What was it, and do you still wish to pursue it? Why or why not? List three major goals you hope to achieve. Describe them in detail, specifying what they are and when you'd like to complete them. Then take action. It's through doing and taking steps that we turn dreams into reality.
	Notes to self:
4	Rise and confront your fear directly. Remind yourself that you possess the strength to triumph. Affirm that you have the bravery necessary to achieve your goals. Resolve from this moment to concentrate on the results of your efforts and build the inner resilience needed to progress.
	Notes to self:
5	Consider the last time you blamed someone. Were you partly responsible? Did you acknowledge your role? If it really was

	their fault, could you have guided them toward improvement instead of placing blame? Start accepting full responsibility for your actions and attitude.
	Notes to self:
6	Assess the leadership you offer your team or those who look up to you. Reflect on how effectively you've supported their development. Think about who currently works with you. Who can you mentor? If they have a positive attitude, share your time, knowledge, and expertise with them.
	Notes to self:
7	Evaluate your current pace. Reflect on both your professional and personal life. Are you progressing at a speed that aligns with your goals for success? Assess your circumstances thoughtfully. Identify three areas where you can pick up the pace. Then accelerate your journey toward success.
	Notes to self:

CHAPTER 10

FIND FULFILLMENT AND HAPPINESS

Remember that the happiest people are not those getting more, but those giving more.

~ H. Jackson Brown Jr. ~

Reflecting on the reasons behind our actions is crucial. This book focuses on developing a strong personal magnetism that allows us to use our charisma to draw in outstanding individuals as we accomplish significant goals. This journey leads to personal satisfaction and joy derived from the influence we then have on the world.

As I reflect on my journey toward personal fulfillment and happiness, I am reminded of a powerful lesson: true happiness is not found in material possessions or fleeting moments of success but in the purpose and meaning we find in our daily lives. This chapter delves into the essence of fulfillment and the pursuit of happiness as I share the insights and experiences that have shaped my understanding of these profound concepts.

From my own experiences, I've come to understand the transient nature of happiness derived from external achievements. Whether it's the thrill of purchasing a new car or the joy of receiving a long-awaited promotion, these moments, though exhilarating, often leave us yearning for something more. This realization led me to explore deeper and seek a more enduring source of fulfillment.

One significant discovery on this journey was the power of living for a purpose greater than oneself. Engaging in acts of kindness and contributing to the well-being of others opened my eyes to a different kind of happiness, one that is both fulfilling and sustainable. The joy that comes from helping others and making a positive impact on the world cannot be overstated. As this book is about making meaningful connections as one attracts others, it is important to realize the central purpose: having positive impacts on others.

I also learned the importance of gratitude and a positive outlook. Life is full of challenges, highs, and lows, but maintaining a grateful heart and finding reasons to appreciate the present moment transforms our experience of life. Gratitude is a powerful catalyst for happiness, turning what we have into more than enough.

In exploring these themes, I realized that the journey of personal growth and self-improvement is as crucial as the destination itself. It's not just about reaching our goals but about who we become along the way. The character we develop, the resilience we build, and the wisdom we gain are the true markers of a fulfilling life.

This chapter is an invitation to join me in this exploration of happiness and fulfillment. It's a call to look beyond the surface, to find joy in your life's journey, and to live with a sense of purpose and gratitude. In this chapter, let us together uncover the secrets to a life of deeper meaning and lasting happiness.

The Only Road to Happiness

One of my favorite movies is the 2006 drama film *Pursuit of Happyness,* starring Will Smith. The movie serves as a reminder that we are all pursuing happiness. This is why you frequently hear people say, "I just want to be happy." But how many people are genuinely happy? Perhaps the better question is, "Are you happy?" Most people experience temporary happiness when something positive happens, such as buying a new car, getting a promotion, welcoming a new child, getting married, or enjoying happy hour on a Friday. Unfortunately, happiness derived from things and events is often fleeting. For instance, drinking wine may make someone temporarily happy, but they return to their previous state once the effects fade.

The reality is that no one can drink themselves into lasting happiness, nor can they dance away their sorrow. If having plenty of money was necessary for happiness, you would need to continually acquire large sums every day for the rest of your life, and even then, true peace and happiness might still elude you. Some people believe that others can make them happy. They think, "If I can just get married" or "If I have great friends, I'll be happy." That might be, but it will only be for a short time. In my observation, truly happy people find their happiness within themselves. Relying on a specific person for your happiness sets you up for significant disappointment, since it's unlikely they'll always keep you happy. Likewise, if you can't be happy with little, achieving much won't necessarily make you happy either.

In May 2022, I toured the Los Angeles area with my family, visiting top destinations like Hollywood and Beverly Hills. We stood on one side of the hill at Griffith Observatory, gazing at Hollywood in all its splendor, the Hollywood sign adorning the hillside. We later strolled through some of the most expensive neighborhoods in America. But does living in Hollywood or Beverly Hills make people happier? Aren't people fundamentally the same everywhere?

No amount of wealth can buy happiness. Riches do not guarantee it. You might own the finest cars, build a mansion lined with gold in an exotic location, feast on gourmet meals, and sip the best wines yet still not find happiness. Likewise, living modestly, envying the wealthy, leading a religious life, and being sanctimonious doesn't necessarily lead to happiness.

Consider having connections with influential people in society. Some believe they will achieve happiness this way. Meaningful relationships are beneficial, particularly when they involve positive influences. However, simply knowing or being connected to well-known individuals doesn't assure happiness. Often, trying to fit into certain social circles causes turmoil as people strive to meet unrelenting standards and constantly compare themselves to others.

Happiness can neither be bought nor created; it must be found or discovered. How do you discover happiness? By living for a purpose greater than yourself. True happiness emerges only when you live for a cause beyond your personal interests. This creates an overwhelming feeling of joy. As *New York Times* bestseller H. Jackson Brown Jr. said, "Remember that the happiest people are not those getting more, but those giving more." A sense of emptiness prevails when we focus solely on ourselves but lack the fulfillment that comes from selflessness.

You might wonder, "How do I live for a purpose greater than myself?" It's simple. Engage in good deeds. Use your talents, resources, and efforts to serve others. Concentrate on the value you contribute to the world. Be generous with what you can offer and perform it with a spirit of service to humanity. It's about living for something larger than oneself. It's about aligning your ultimate purpose with serving humanity. By doing so, you discover happiness.

Moreover, it is essential to recognize that doing good is a profitable endeavor. Have you ever questioned when your acts of kindness will be returned? Do you sometimes feel discouraged, thinking you've given a lot but received little? You're not alone. Yet millions of good-doers also invest their energy and resources in uplifting others and society without necessarily expecting anything in return.

Without comprehending the true purpose of doing good, one might become weary and consider ceasing their efforts. Genuine good-doers generally don't expect much, if anything, in return. They engage in good deeds for the sake of goodness itself. They discover a greater purpose in doing good, even without the expectation of recompense.

When we perform good deeds, we experience a sense of fulfillment and contentment. We feel joy knowing we have sown something that may eventually bring a harvest, regardless of personal benefit. Good deeds can take various forms. You might spend time and resources helping others, be a caring parent, provide training and mentorship, contribute positively at work, exemplify strong character and moral judgment, or dedicate your life to serving humanity.

Whatever good you do, remember it is a profitable endeavor. The path to happiness and contentment is lined with good deeds and a sincere heart dedicated to serving humanity.

Be the Spreader of Joy

"No matter how gloomy the cloud may be, there will still be a silver lining." Though this expression of wisdom has different variations around the world, it was part of my upbringing. Often, we focus on what's going wrong and neglect the positives. It's common to notice our problems while disregarding all our blessings. Being mindful of our pain is natural, but it's easy to overlook moments of peace. This tendency shapes our general outlook on life.

We unconsciously project our struggles and frustrations, and this occasionally results in negative impacts. Unhappy individuals cannot spread happiness. Those who dwell solely on their pain are unlikely to bring joy to others. It's not about whether we face challenges but how our attitude influences our ultimate experience.

One key realization is that no matter how challenging situations become, there's always something to be thankful for. Instead of focusing our energy on shortcomings, we should concentrate on what brings us joy. A joyful heart radiates light to others. Edith Wharton's quote from *Vesalius in Zante,* "There are two ways of spreading light: to be the candle or the mirror that reflects it," encapsulates this idea. Our true life experience stems from our hearts. When the heart is in the right place, everything falls into place. Conversely, a heart filled with bitterness sees nothing as right. The state of our heart depends on our perspective and attitude rather than external events.

It appears that each of us must make a choice. Life presents various challenges, some negative. Ups and downs are a reality for everyone. Instead of letting life's trials steal our joy, we should allow goodness to flow from within. Consequently, our true experience relies not on external circumstances but on inner strength. Let your heart glow. Be a source of joy.

There is Something Better Than Achievements

It's always thrilling to experience the euphoria that accompanies significant achievements. Think back to your feelings when you graduated from college, bought a home or car, completed an important task, met a specific goal, or made a notable accomplishment. You felt joy and triumph. But what came next? How did the achievement affect you beyond the initial excitement? What was its deeper significance to you?

I recall the day I earned my doctorate. It felt incredible to move from being in the audience to being on stage with my certificate in hand. People began addressing me as "Doctor." However, I questioned whether anything had truly changed for me. Was there a tangible difference before and after obtaining the degree?

Then it hit me. The essence is not solely about the achievement itself. It's about who we become while we strive to reach that achievement. Is standing on Mount Everest the ultimate goal for the climber? Not exactly. They celebrate the effort, courage, resilience, determination, and will to succeed that it took to achieve that goal. In other words, the essence of the joy stemming from the achievement is the person they evolve into during the journey, not the achievement itself.

The most crucial part of our accomplishments is the growth and lessons learned along the way. The process makes us more robust and better prepared for future challenges. US Supreme Court Justice Oliver Wendell Holmes's words, "A mind that is stretched by a new experience can never go back to its old dimensions," emphasize this idea.

This book examines how to become the kind of individual others aspire to be around and how to master the art of attracting like-minded people while pursuing significant life achievements. Think about your relationships and those who have crossed your path. Consider the individuals you have drawn in or will attract due to your appealing personality. The overarching goal is to become a person of substance and value, improving yourself in the process.

Here's the key takeaway: Who you become during your journey is more critical than what you achieve. That should motivate you to aim high. Your drive to accomplish remarkable things must lay the groundwork for an outstanding character. Striving for excellence transforms you, enabling you to serve humanity in the best way possible.

When the Whole World Sings Your Praises

Consider the analogy of the proverbial clay pot. The clay pot excelled in its role and was highly regarded. For instance, when an elephant dies, people use the clay pot to collect its meat for cooking, allowing them to enjoy many meals. Similarly, they used the clay pot to hold buffalo meat and soup and more. However, when the clay pot died, in other words broke, it was discarded and forgotten. This scenario often reflects reality, reminding us that we must be prepared for the eventuality of losing influence or fame. Many former celebrities and powerful figures still live among us, but they no longer hold the same recognition as they did during their peak.

There are several reasons individuals may receive praise, such as notable achievements, fame, stardom, and holding positions of authority. Nonetheless, since everything is transient, it is crucial to remember that once the cause for acclaim vanishes, so does the praise.

One might argue, "What if I consistently perform excellently, ensuring my glory endures?" My response it that it's important to understand that the praise is not genuinely about you but rather about what you possess. Your true essence is reflected by who you are beyond fame and power. After your departure, people may not recall your achievement but will certainly remember your character. Instead of allowing praise to inflate our egos, we should remain dedicated to our initial mission, which is the root of our fame and authority. It all boils down to genuine humility, being humble in spirit and manifesting humility through our actions.

Here is the core message: We should never bring ourselves down due to pride or arrogance. It is overly self-confident and even arrogant to believe that admiration stems solely from your merit. In reality, people praise you because of your fame, wealth, and power. If you think this perspective is hypothetical, just observe how many people remain once you no longer possess those attributes. Most will desert you, save for a few who truly care— if you are fortunate to have created such bonds on your journey to your achievement as mentioned earlier.

When the world sings your praises, maintain humility throughout and concentrate on your mission and good deeds. That is what history will remember. As Pastor Rick Warren wisely stated, "Humility is not thinking less of yourself, it's thinking of yourself less." Embracing humility is one of the keys to enduring happiness and fulfillment.

Ensure You Will Not Be Quickly Forgotten

Our lives are a collection of unique stories interconnected over time. Everyone's life narrative is distinct; your biography will differ from mine because we are each unique. While everyone's journey is different, some people will leave enduring legacies, while others may fade from memory. Consider this: certain individuals create lasting impressions in the hearts of others, while many pass through life without leaving a lasting impact or memorable traces.

In my book, *Pursuit of Personal Leadership,* I detailed how we can consciously incorporate elements into our daily lives that will become our legacies. I provided numerous examples that serve as valuable lessons. Crafting an unforgettable life story is straightforward. If you aspire to be remembered for something, actively work toward it. One way to achieve a lasting legacy is to engage in actions that transcend self-interest and hold long-term value. Although I cannot define what this means for you, I am confident that each of us has the potential to make a lasting impact. Reflect on the lives of those who have dedicated themselves to serving humanity. Your contribution may not be as remarkable as that of Mother Teresa's, but you can certainly support a cause, build a legacy, help others, or establish something new that endures beyond your lifetime.

Those who live self-centered lives are often quickly forgotten, while those who positively affect others are remembered for writing their stories in the hearts of others. As Benjamin Franklin said, "If you would not be forgotten as soon as you are dead and rotten, either write something worth reading, or do something worth writing." However, remember that our stories should bring about good rather than harm. When crafting your life story, aim to create one that fosters happiness, goodwill, and benefits for others. To ensure you are not easily forgotten, write a story that endures and leaves a meaningful legacy.

CHAPTER 10 SUMMARY

True fulfillment and lasting legacies come from humility, meaningful actions, and contributions that benefit others rather than from transient fame or material success. By focusing on our purpose, engaging in acts of kindness, and maintaining a grateful heart, we can ensure that our impact endures and brings about enduring happiness and positive influence. This chapter can be summarized as follows:

1. True happiness is found in purpose and meaning, not in material possessions or fleeting moments of success.

2. Engaging in acts of kindness and contributing to the well-being of others leads to fulfilling and sustainable happiness.
3. Gratitude transforms our experience of life, turning what we have into enough.
4. The journey of personal growth and self-improvement is as important as reaching goals, which shapes our character and resilience.
5. Happiness comes from living for a purpose greater than oneself and performing good deeds without expecting anything in return.
6. A joyful heart radiates and spreads light to others, which positively influences our overall life experience.
7. The person we become during our journey is more important than the achievements themselves, which emphasizes growth and self-improvement.
8. Maintaining humility is crucial when receiving praise, so we must focus on our mission and good deeds rather than personal ego.
9. Creating a lasting legacy involves engaging in actions that transcend self-interest and hold long-term value.

CHAPTER 10 REFLECTIONS FOR ACTION

It's time to act on what you have learned in this chapter. Kindly read the reflection questions in the following table, and in the space provided, note what actions you will take and when.

	Reflection Questions
1	When you've purchased something new, such as a car or a pair of shoes, how long did the happiness last? What has been the happiest moment in your life? Have you managed to maintain that happiness? Why or why not?

Notes to self:

2	Assess your good-doing level. Is it simple or challenging for you to perform acts of kindness or help others and society? Reflect on this. Then plan a significant act of kindness without expecting any reward and carry it out.
	Notes to self:
3	Choose to remain calm and satisfied with your life, even if you haven't acquired everything you desire. Seek out reasons to be thankful in all situations. Cultivate gratitude.
	Notes to self:
4	Think about some of the most memorable moments in your life. What insights did you gain from those experiences? How have significant achievements contributed to shaping your identity?
	Notes to self:

5	Reflect on your current situation, regardless of whether you have attained stardom or significant influence. Do you consider yourself humble? Evaluate yourself and commit to ensuring that no achievement, recognition, or praise hampers your humility. Always think and act with humility.
	Notes to self:
6	Identify three attributes or achievements you want to be remembered for. Next, outline the steps required to realize them. Finally, take action and begin building your legacy.
	Notes to self:

CONCLUSION

As I conclude this book, I'm reflecting on the journey we've taken together. Throughout these pages, I've shared insights and experiences that have shaped my understanding of personal magnetism and the qualities that make an individual truly captivating. The essence of this book lies in the belief that anyone can cultivate a personality that draws others in, not through superficial means but by nurturing inner qualities that make us genuinely appealing.

I've emphasized the importance of graciousness, self-improvement, and the power of presence. These are not just abstract concepts but actionable ones that can transform how we interact with the world. By being kind, patient, and resilient, we can build meaningful connections and inspire those around us. It's about exuding confidence and self-belief, recalibrating our mindset, and embracing creativity and innovation.

The journey to personal magnetism is continuous. It requires a commitment to continuous growth and a willingness to face challenges with grace and determination. It's about leading with integrity, being thoughtful in our actions, and maintaining a positive attitude even in the face of adversity. As we strive to become better versions of ourselves, we naturally attract others who are drawn to our authenticity and strength of character.

In writing this book, my hope is that I inspire you to embark on your own journey of personal growth, to see the potential within yourself, and to take the steps necessary to unlock it. Remember, the power to captivate and inspire lies within you. It's a journey worth taking, and I am honored to have been a part of it. Thank you for allowing me to share my thoughts and experiences with you. May you find fulfillment and happiness as you continue to cultivate your own personal magnetism.

I hope you have been inspired by this book and that you enjoyed every page. I would like to ask you to kindly leave a review or rating wherever you acquired the book or simply go to Amazon, type the book title, and leave a review.

Let us connect.

www.deleola.com | LinkedIn | @TheDeleOla on Twitter & Instagram

ABOUT THE AUTHOR

Dr. Dele Ola is an award-winning author, an accomplished professional engineer and scientist, and a change leader with a profound level of experience in corporate circles and a strong voice in the leadership development community. He started his career in the technology consulting industry in a global Fortune-500 company before transitioning into the Canadian applied research system. He has served in various leadership positions within Canada's innovation ecosystem and on the board of several prominent organizations.

Dr. Ola holds a doctorate degree in mechanical engineering from the University of Manitoba. He is a certified lean six-sigma practitioner, a program manager, a published scientist, a technology executive, and a prolific writer of leadership literature. His book, *Be A Change Agent: Leadership in a Time of Exponential Change*, won the business category of the 2021 Next Generation Indie Book Awards and has a growing readership around the world. He is also the author of other successful books including *Pursuit of Personal Leadership: Practical Principles of Personal Achievement* and *Rip Off Your Blindfold: See How Successful People See*.

Dr. Ola is passionate about leadership, personal growth, skills development, and technological innovation. An active leader in innovation and applied research, Dr. Ola continues to lead change in his work and the world. His vision is to develop change agents to challenge the status quo, take charge of the future, and evolve into what they are meant to be in life.

NOTES

Chapter 1: Radiate a Captivating Presence

1. "John Wesley > Quotes > Quotable Quote," Goodreads, accessed November 8, 2024, https://www.goodreads.com/quotes/576772-we-should-be-rigorous-in-judging-ourselves-and-gracious-in
2. "Madonna > Quotes > Quotable Quote," Goodreads, accessed November 8, 2024, https://www.goodreads.com/quotes/110225-no-matter-who-you-are-no-matter-what-you-did
3. "Viktor E. Frankl > Quotes > Quotable Quote," Goodreads, accessed November 8, 2024, https://www.goodreads.com/quotes/52939-when-we-are-no-longer-able-to-change-a-situation
4. "Abigail Van Buren > Quotes > Quotable Quote," Goodreads, accessed on November 8, 2024, https://www.goodreads.com/quotes/9940-the-best-index-to-a-person-s-character-is-how-he
5. "Eleanor Roosevelt," National Archives: Franklin D. Roosevelt Presidential Library and Museum, accessed November 11, 2024, https://www.fdrlibrary.org/eleanor-roosevelt
6. "35 Inspirational Wayne Dyer Quotes to Help You Live an Extraordinary Life," The Strive, accessed November 11, 2024, https://thestrive.co/wayne-dyer-quotes/

Chapter 2: Recalibrate Your Mindset and Attitude

1. "Dale Carnegie > Quotes > Quotable Quote," Goodreads, accessed November 11, 2024, https://www.goodreads.com/quotes/10749-most-of-the-important-things-in-the-world-have-been
2. "Plato," Bartleby, accessed November 11, 2024, https://www.bartleby.com/lit-hub/forty-thousand-quotations-prose-and-poetical/authors/plato-8
3. "Bruce Lee > Quotes > Quotable Quote," Goodreads, accessed November 11, 2024, https://www.goodreads.com/quotes/9087407-absorb-what-is-useful-discard-what-is-not-add-what
4. "Joyce Brothers > Quotes > Quotable Quote," Goodreads, accessed November 11, 2024, https://www.goodreads.com/quotes/42749-success-is-a-state-of-mind-if-you-want-success
5. "The Socratic Method," n.a., accessed November 11, 2024, https://www.socratic-method.com/quote-meanings-interpretations/martin-luther-king-jr-we-must-accept-finite-disappointment-but-never-lose-infinite-hope-2
6. Dickens, C., & Sharp, W., *The old curiosity shop* (Heritage Press, 1941).
7. "W. Clement Stone > Quotes," Goodreads, accessed November 11, 2024, https://www.goodreads.com/author/quotes/46897.W_Clement_Stone
8. Charles Dickens, *Bleak House* (Penguin Books, 2003)
9. Rick Warren, *The Purpose Driven Life: What On Earth Am I Here For?* (Zondervan 2013)

Chapter 3: Exude Self-Belief and Confidence

1. "Tim Fargo > Quotes > Quotable Quote," Goodreads, accessed November 9, 2024, https://www.goodreads.com/quotes/1384112-if-you-want-to-improve-your-self-worth-stop-giving-other
2. "The Socratic Method," n.a., accessed November 9, 2024, https://www.socratic-method.com/quote-meanings/nelson-mandela-there-is-no-passion-to-be-found-playing-small-in-settling-for-a-life-that-is-less-than-the-one-you-are-capable-of-living
3. Nathaniel Hawthorne, *The Scarlet Letter* (Signet Classic, 1988)
4. "Henry Ford > Quotes > Quotable Quote," Goodreads, accessed November 9, 2024, https://www.goodreads.com/quotes/45227-there-is-no-man-living-who-isn-t-capable-of-doing
5. "State of the Union February 6, 1985," Ronal Reagan Presidential Foundation & Institute, accessed November 9, 2024, https://www.reaganfoundation.org/ronald-reagan/reagan-quotes-speeches/state-of-the-union-3/
6. "Dale Carnegie > Quotes > Quotable Quote," Goodreads, accessed November 9, 2024, https://www.goodreads.com/quotes/450949-inaction-breeds-doubt-and-fear-action-breeds-confidence-and-courage
7. George Eliot, *Middlemarch: A Study of Provincial Life* (New American Library, 1964)
8. Tony Robbins, *Awaken The Giant Within* (Simon and Schuster, 2012)

Chapter 4: Use the Power of Presence to Build Meaningful Connections

1. Mike McIntyre, *The Kindness of Strangers: Penniless Across America* (Berkley Books, 1996)
2. John Wesley, "The Use of Money," What Saith the Scripture? Accessed November 11, 2024, https://www.whatsaiththescripture.com/Text.Only/pdfs/The_Use_of_Money_Text.pdf
3. "No One Can Whistle a Symphony, It Takes an Orchestra to Play It," John Murphy International, accessed November 11, 2024, https://johnmurphyinternational.com/blog/no-one-can-whistle-a-symphony-it-takes-an-orchestra-to-play-it/
4. Stephen R. Covey, *The 7 Habits of Highly Effective People: Restoring the Character Ethic* (Simon and Schuster, 1989)
5. Neale Donald Walsch, *Conversations with God: An Uncommon Dialogue 1st ed.* (G.P. Putnam's Sons, 1995)
6. Morgan L. Busse, *Secrets in the Mist* (Enclave Escape, 2021)
7. "70 Helping others quotes that'll inspire doing good deeds," Bliss Quote, accessed November 11, 2024, https://www.blissquote.com/2019/08/helping-others-quotes.html
8. "Henri Frederic Amiel Quotes," AZ Quotes, accessed November 11, 2024, https://www.azquotes.com/author/349-Henri_Frederic_Amiel

Chapter 5: Embrace Success in All Facets of Life

1. "The Art of Worldly Wisdom, by Baltasar Gracián (1601-1658) translated by Joseph Jacobs (1892)," Monadnock Valley Press, accessed November 9, 2024, https://monadnock.net/gracian/wisdom.html

2. "A New Perspective: 67 Quotes About Being Open Minded," Subconscious Servant, accessed November 9, 2024, https://subconsciousservant.com/open-minded-quotes/
3. "Debasish Mridha > Quotes > Quotable Quote," Goodreads, accessed November 9, 2024, https://www.goodreads.com/quotes/9120627-life-is-a-daring-adventure-towards-an-unknown-future-its
4. "Alex Wek Quotes," BrainyQuote, accessed November 9, 2024, https://www.brainyquote.com/quotes/alek_wek_783092
5. "Top 10 Charlotte Rae Quotes," BrainyQuote, accessed November 9, 2024, https://www.brainyquote.com/lists/authors/top-10-charlotte-rae-quotes

Chapter 6: Let Your Creativity and Innovation Speak

1. "William Faulkner > Quotes > Quotable Quote," Goodreads, accessed November 11, 2024, https://www.goodreads.com/quotes/132400-you-cannot-swim-for-new-horizons-until-you-have-courage
2. Washington Irving, *The Legend of Sleepy Hollow and Other Stories*, (Chartwell Books, 2022)
3. "Audrey Hepburn > Quotes > Quotable Quote," Goodreads, accessed November 11, 2024, https://www.goodreads.com/quotes/831377-to-plant-a-garden-is-to-believe-in-tomorrow
4. "Brian Tracy > Quotes > Quotable Quote," Goodreads, accessed November 11, 2024, https://www.goodreads.com/quotes/22987-i-ve-found-that-luck-is-quite-predictable-if-you-want
5. "10 of Laura Ingalls Wilder's most inspiring quotes," American Masters, accessed November 11, 2024,

https://www.pbs.org/wnet/americanmasters/10-of-laura-ingalls-wilders-most-inspiring-quotes/16174/
6. "Alvin Toffler > Quotes > Quotable Quote," Goodreads, accessed November 11, 2024, https://www.goodreads.com/quotes/313653-you-ve-got-to-think-about-big-things-while-you-re-doing

Chapter 7: Be an Overcomer

1. "13 Prosperity Quotes from Randy Gage," Prime Concepts Creative Marketing Agency, accessed November 8, 2024, https://primeconcepts.com/randy-gage-quotes/
2. Napoleon Hill, *Think and Grow Rich 1st ed.* (Ballantine Books, 1983)
3. Roy T. Bennett, *The Light in the Heart: Inspirational Thoughts for Living Your Best Life,* (Roy Bennett, 2016)
4. "The Socratic Method," n.a., accessed November 8, 2024, https://www.socratic-method.com/quote-meanings/napoleon-bonaparte-impossible-is-a-word-to-be-found-only-in-the-dictionary-of-fools
5. "Mandy Hale > Quotes > Quotable Quote," Goodreads, accessed November 8, 2024, https://www.goodreads.com/quotes/1023321-growth-is-painful-change-is-painful-but-nothing-is-as
6. Jack Canfield, *The Success Principles: How to Get from Where You Are to Where You Want to Be* (HarperCollins, 2005)
7. "Mario Cuomo Quotes," AZ Quotes, accessed November 8, 2024, https://www.azquotes.com/author/3503-Mario_Cuomo
8. "The Socratic Method," n.a., accessed November 8, 2024, https://www.socratic-method.com/quote-meanings/jimmy-dean-i-

cant-change-the-direction-of-the-wind-but-i-can-adjust-my-sails-to-always-reach-my-destination
9. Steve Maraboli, *Life, the Truth, and Being Free* (Better Today, 2009)

Chapter 8: Become an Efficient Self-Manager

1. Stephen R. Covey, *The 7 Habits of Highly Effective People: Restoring the Character Ethic* (Simon and Schuster, 1989)
2. "Many people fail in life, not for lack of ability or brains or even courage but simply because they have never organized their energies around a goal, Elbert Hubbard," AZ Quotes, accessed November 23, 2024, https://www.azquotes.com/quote/556133
3. "The Trouble With Not Having a Goal …," LIFEHACKER, accessed November 23, 2024, https://lifehacker.com/the-trouble-with-not-having-a-goal-5868799
4. Holly Lisle, *Gods Old and Dark* (HarperCollins, 2009)
5. "Brené Brown > Quotes > Quotable Quote," Goodreads, accessed November 23, 2024, https://www.goodreads.com/quotes/641983-if-you-own-this-story-you-get-to-write-the
6. Calvin Coolidge, "Law and Order," recorded March 2, 1920, New York, in American Leaders Speak: Recordings from World War I, Library of Congress, copy of a 78 rpm disk, 4 min., 40 sec., https://lccn.loc.gov/2004650650
7. "50 Slow Down Quotes to Enjoy Life," Positive Thinking Mind, accessed November 23, 2024, https://positivethinkingmind.com/50-slow-down-quotes-to-enjoy-life/

Chapter 9: Be Patient but Persist

1. "The Key to Everything is Patience. You Get the Chicken by Hatching the Egg, Not by Smashing it, Arnold H. Glasow," #PassItOn, accessed November 11, 2024, https://www.passiton.com/inspirational-quotes/7727-the-key-to-everything-is-patience-you-get-the
2. "Jeanette Coron > Quotes > Quotable Quote," Goodreads, accessed November 11, 2024, https://www.goodreads.com/quotes/7390417-the-greater-the-destiny-the-greater-obstacles-you-ll-have-to
3. "Douglas Everett > Quotes > Quotable Quote," Goodreads, accessed November 11, 2024, https://www.goodreads.com/quotes/25367-there-are-some-people-who-live-in-a-dream-world
4. Nelson Mandela, *Long Walk To Freedom: The Autobiography of Nelson Mandela* (Little; Brown, 1984)
5. "Leading Thoughts," Leadership Now: Building a Community of Leaders, accessed November 11, 2024, https://leadershipnow.com/responsibilityquotes.html
6. Jack Welch & Suzy Welch, *Winning* (Harper Business, 2005)
7. "Charles M. Schulz > Quotes > Quotable Quote," Goodreads, accessed November 11, 2024, https://www.quotespedia.org/authors/c/charles-m-schulz/life-is-like-a-ten-speed-bicycle-most-of-us-have-gears-we-never-use-charles-m-schulz/

Chapter 10: Find Fulfillment and Happiness

1. "Remember that the happiest people are not those getting more, but those giving more, H. Jackson Brown Jr.," AZ Quotes, accessed November 23, 2024, https://www.azquotes.com/quote/38138
2. Edith Wharton, "Vesalius in Zante (1564)," *North American Review, 175* (1902): 625-631
3. Oliver Wendell Holmes Sr., "The Autocrat of the Breakfast-Table," *The Atlantic Monthly* (Sept. 1858):
4. Rick Warren, *The Purpose Driven Life: What On Earth am I Here For?* (Zondervan, 2013)
5. "Poor Richard's Almanack Quotes," Goodreads, accessed January 10, 2025, https://www.goodreads.com/work/quotes/1957101-poor-richards-almanack

About Dr. Dele Ola's Award-Winning *Be a Change Agent*

Are you painfully aware of the mismatch between outdated approaches and our rapidly evolving world? Dr. Dele Ola looks unflinchingly at the problem of resisting change and offers a wealth of expert guidance on how to embrace positive growth and foster development.

Be A Change Agent is a comprehensive examination of change leadership: the need for it, the qualities of change leaders, and the importance of having great change teams. Dr. Ola first guides the reader through stories of fearless leaders and explores the Veritas qualities that made them successful. Then he discusses building collaborative teams that work well and have the independence to innovate without overt bureaucratic control. Dr. Ola's years working with high-performance teams helped him develop an insightful tool for looking at three spectrums that cause tension in teams:

- The Systems Spectrum-Structure versus influence
- The Reaction Spectrum-Reflection versus action
- The Perspective Spectrum-Reality versus idealism

And the Tensions Equalizer tool will change how you view the balance of members in your team. Finally, the book culminates in a discussion of the future of work, learning, enterprise, and innovation.

Complete with insightful questionnaires and reflection questions, *Be A Change Agent* offers a practical toolkit for both emerging change agents and seasoned influencers to evaluate their leadership qualities and become the very best they can be.

About Dr. Dele Ola's *Pursuit of Personal Leadership*

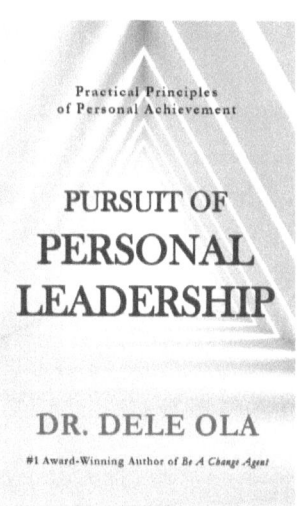

The definition of success and personal achievement is not universal as success comes in different shapes and sizes and at different life stages for everyone. For those looking at where they are and where they want to be and wondering how to get there, do not look any further. Using real-life examples, Dr. Dele Ola presents proven, practicable, and timeless principles to guide you on your journey to great achievements, a journey he calls "the pursuit of personal leadership."

Dr. Ola has learned that you can only attract great achievements and make great impacts through a process of personal change and imbibing the culture and discipline of successful people. The world must make room for someone who has discovered, and has the desire and determination, to develop and exploit their gifts, talents, and abilities to establish themselves in what they have determined to be their exact purpose and calling in life.

In *Pursuit of Personal Leadership*, Dr. Ola highlights a missing piece in leadership literature, which is the discovery of one's personal identity. He explains the need for a personal blueprint for success and how to develop your blueprint. Learn how to cultivate the necessary personal leadership attitudes, exploit your creativity, discover and establish your life's work, explore the world of possibilities, and understand the five seasons of personal leadership every successful person experiences.

Most importantly, all successful agents of change should understand and embrace the responsibilities of modeling success and leaving a legacy.

About Dr. Dele Ola's *Rip Off Your Blindfold*

Using the terrifying real-life example of driving through foggy weather on a highway as a platform, Dr. Dele Ola teaches us that the true definition of blindness is lack of insight, perception, or judgment. Many people go through life working hard but never seeing results because they don't see clearly. They go through life as if they're driving through the fog or wearing a blindfold.

This is why abuse of authority in corporations and politics exists. This is why society doesn't function optimally, why there is dysfunctional leadership at all levels, and why many people fail in their personal and professional lives.

What we see is a function of our eyesight; *how* we see is a function of our insight. We must acquire clear-sightedness to succeed. Successful people leave a mark, experience personal fulfillment, and change the world because they see through their insight rather than their eyesight. The mind sees much more, and much farther, than the eyes can. You can see the world clearly through your mind without eyesight, but you cannot see clearly without insight.

Captivating stories and personal anecdotes illustrate the central theme: we need to remove the barriers to clear-sightedness, the dense fog that beclouds understanding and prevents people from leading effectively, running successful businesses, accomplishing great things, reaching personal goals, and fulfilling personal visions.

Dr. Ola himself strives to always live the principles presented in this book. He cites several examples from his own life and the lives of others throughout. Given his firm belief that one of the worst flaws anyone can have is to possess physical sight but lack insight and be unable to see the world clearly through the lens of sound principles, Dr. Ola passionately shares how to see clearly with insight for the betterment of ourselves and our world.